THE MARSHALL CAVENDISH

☆ ☆ ☆ ILLUSTRATED ☆ ☆ ☆

ENCYCLOPEDIA OF

WORLD WAR II

VOLUME 9

THE MARSHALL CAVENDISH
☆ ☆ ☆ ILLUSTRATED ☆ ☆ ☆
ENCYCLOPEDIA OF

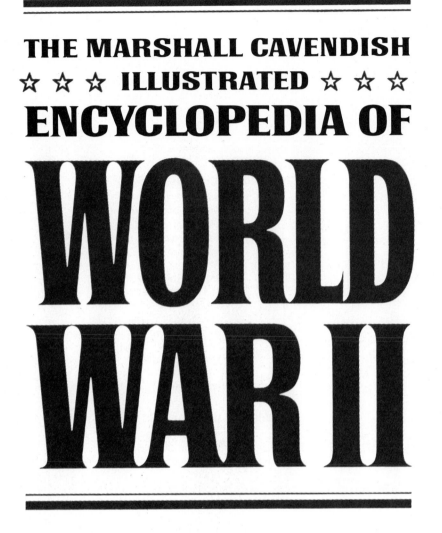

WORLD WAR II

Based on the original text by
Lieutenant Colonel Eddy Bauer

CONSULTANT EDITOR

Brigadier General James L. Collins, Jr., U.S.A.

CHIEF OF MILITARY HISTORY,
DEPARTMENT OF THE ARMY

MARSHALL CAVENDISH CORPORATION/NEW YORK

CONTENTS

Editorial Director: Brian Innes
Editor-in-chief; Brigadier Peter Young, D.S.O., M.C., M.A.
Managing Editor: Richard Humble
Editor: Christopher Chant
Art Editor: Jim Bridge

CHAPTER 82

Casablanca conference

On November 10, 1942 Winston Churchill was the chief guest at the Lord Mayor's traditional banquet at the Mansion House. When he was called on to give his address, he commented on the recent successes of Anglo-American strategy from El Alamein to Operation "Torch". At the close of his speech, which Sir Alan Brooke described as "very good", the Prime Minister said, cautiously and with some reserve:

"This must not be considered as the end; it may possibly be the beginning of the end, but it certainly is the end of the beginning."

But the British and American Governments still had to discuss how and where to exploit these considerable successes; they had to decide whether they should keep to the plan made in London at the end of July 1942, according to which Operation "Round-up" would follow Operation "Torch" in the summer of 1943. This was the purpose of the Casablanca Conference, which was attended by Roosevelt, Churchill, and their staffs, from January 14 to 23, 1942.

▽ America's presence in North Africa— U.S. flag bearers at attention in front of President Roosevelt's villa at Casablanca during the week of January 17, 1943.

△△ *Churchill at the microphone during the Mansion House banquet of November 10, 1942, commenting on the initial success of the "American landings" in North Africa. The gist of the speech was "This must not be considered as the end; it may possibly be the beginning of the end, but it certainly is the end of the beginning."*

△ *Pious American expectations · for moves against Hitler in 1943.*

article in the *Revue d'histoire moderne et contemporaine* in 1963, the British and Americans have maintained their positions and since 1945 have not drawn any closer together in their views of the conference.

Priority for "Torch"

"In short, what is it all about?" Marshal Foch used to say. If we asked the same question about the Casablanca debate we could answer as follows:

Did Winston Churchill and the chiefs of the British General Staff deliberately make use of the same deceptive methods in dealing with their American partners as they had when they withdrew from their obligations to open a second front in Europe, in the autumn of 1942, between the time of Hopkins' and General Marshall's first visit to London in April 1942 and their return there in July?

On the other hand, the question arises whether the British deliberated for a considerable period before they managed to convince their allies that the continuation of Operation "Torch" into Sicily and southern Italy was more important than Operation "Round-up". With the documents that we have before us it is not possible to give a straightforward positive or negative answer to these questions.

In his memoirs Winston Churchill states that at the time of the British and American landings in North Africa, he hoped that the Allies would be in possession of all their stated objectives, including the "Tunisian promontory", within a few months.

"In this case the main invasion of Occupied France from England would still be possible in July or August 1943. I was therefore most anxious that the strongest build-up of American power in Britain which our shipping would allow should proceed at the same time as 'Torch'. This idea of being able to use our left as well as our right hand, and the fact that the enemy must prepare himself against blows from either, seemed wholly in accordance with the highest economy of war. Events would decide whether we should thrust across the Channel or follow our luck in the Mediterranean, or both. It seemed imperative, in the interests of the war as a whole and especially of aiding Russia, that the Anglo-American armies should enter Europe either from the west or from

The Anglo-American dispute

Much has been written in Great Britain and the U.S.A. since the end of World War II about the discussions between the Allies at the conference and the decisions which emerged. The American journalist Ralph Ingersoll wrote the first book on the subject, *Ultra Secret*. He wrote in a lively, indeed polemical, style about the war strategy which in his view was imposed by the crafty Churchill on the naïve and innocent Roosevelt. The Australian Chester Wilmot answered this book in January 1952, when he published a large volume entitled *The Struggle for Europe*, which was decidedly in Churchill's favour. In the meantime Robert E. Sherwood had published the papers of Harry Hopkins, the *éminence grise* of the White House, and Churchill himself had written the section of his memoirs dealing with the Casablanca Conference. As was natural and to be expected, the records of the general staffs' historical departments present a carefully balanced picture. However, as J. B. Duroselle of the *Centre d'études des relations internationales* noted perceptively in a well-informed the east in the coming year."

It may be asked whether Churchill in his memoirs pretends to intentions he never had at the time of which he was writing (November 1942), in order to answer his American critics; many writers use such arguments after the event. This is not the case, since in his judgement the conclusions reached by the Chiefs-of-Staff who were making their operational plans for 1943 were "too negative", and he told them so on November 9, 1942, without waiting for the end of Operation "Torch":

"We have already committed ourselves with the Americans to 'Round-up' in 1943, an operation on the greatest scale. The interposition of 'Torch' is no excuse for lying down during 1943, content with descents on Sicily and Sardinia and a few more operations like Dieppe (which can hardly be taken as a pattern).

"The effort for the campaign of 1943 should clearly be a strong pinning down of the enemy in Northern France and the Low Countries by continuous preparations to invade, and a decisive attack in Italy, or better still, Southern France, together with operations not involving serious shipping expense, and other forms of pressure to bring in Turkey and operate overland with the Russians in the Balkans.

"If French North Africa is going to be made an excuse for locking up great forces on the defensive and calling it a 'commitment', it would be better not to have gone there at all. Is it really to be supposed that the Russians will be content with our lying down like this during the whole of 1943, while Hitler has a third crack at them? However alarming the prospect may seem, we must make an attempt to get on to the mainland of Europe and fight in the line against the enemy in 1943."

On November 18 he repeated the same story. Doubtless, as "Torch" was using up 13 divisions, it would only be possible to employ 35 for "Round-up", instead of the 48 previously agreed between the British and the Americans. But for all that it was surely not necessary to throw in the towel after the first setback? He had to admit:

"But there is a frightful gap between what the Chiefs of Staff contemplated as reasonable in the summer of 1942 for the campaign of 1943 and what they now say we can do in the campaign ... No doubt we were planning too much for 1943 in the summer, but we are certainly planning too little now ... We have, in fact, pulled in our horns to an almost extraordinary extent, and I cannot imagine what the Russians will say or do when they realise it. My own position is that I am still aiming at a 'Round-up' retarded till August. I cannot give this up without a massive presentation of facts and figures which prove physical impossibility."

Brooke supports Churchill

Churchill's critics may object that the texts quoted are to some extent used to excuse his actions, and that he presented them to conceal his real thoughts from the reader. However, General Sir Alan Brooke in his diaries has shown that he deeply regretted the fits of "dangerous impatience" which overtook his tempestuous leader at this time.

Certainly Brooke was considerably relieved to hear of the arrival of a convoy of four warships at Malta on November 20, but the news reaching him from Tunisia appeared "rather confused".

Eisenhower and Anderson had not seized the opportunities open to them, and Montgomery, who had reached the El Agheila pass, was held back in his pursuit by heavy rainstorms and logistic difficulties. In this situation it was to be feared that Rommel might partially recover his freedom of action. Winston Churchill, Brooke's "indomitable 'boss'", as Sir Arthur Bryant describes him, therefore took the initiative and overwhelmed his chiefs-of-staff with a continuous stream of proposals for attack:

"November 30th ... C.O.S. at which we examined most recent ideas of P.M. for re-entry into Continent in 1943, and where he is again trying to commit us to a definite plan of action. After lunch interview with Secretary of State on new proposed man-power cuts of P.M. He never faces realities: at one moment we are reducing our forces, and the next we are invading the Continent with vast armies for which there is no hope of ever finding the shipping. He is quite incorrigible and I am quite exhausted ...

"Cabinet meeting from 5.30 to 8 p.m. and now we are off for another meeting with P.M. from 10.30 p.m. to God knows when, to discuss more ambitious and impossible plans for the re-conquest of Burma."

On December 3, when Churchill returned to the subject, Brooke noted in his diary:

"C.O.S. meeting at which we were faced

Air Chief-Marshal Sir Arthur Tedder was born in 1890. He joined the Army in 1913, and after serving in Fiji and in France transferred to the Royal Flying Corps in 1915. After the war Tedder served in Turkey and then attended a course at the Naval War College before holding posts in the Air Ministry. Between 1936 and 1939 he was A.O.C. Far East, and in 1939 was Director of Research and Development at the Air Ministry. After transfer to the Middle East, Tedder was appointed A.O.C. Middle East in May 1941, as which he carefully built up and trained his command into a superb tactical air force, which won final mastery of the North African skies in time for the Battle of El Alamein. As a result of the Casablanca Conference, Tedder became Allied Air Commander in the Mediterranean. Eisenhower, impressed by Tedder's strategic abilities, made him Deputy Supreme Commander for the invasion of North-West Europe.

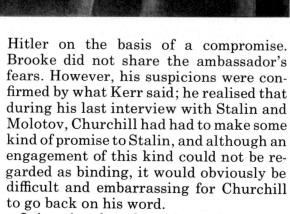

△ Operation "Torch" and the subsequent course of events in North Africa provided the Axis powers with striking proof that the "United Nations", the concept of which was so beloved by Roosevelt, was a viable and increasingly powerful entity.

with a new paper by the P.M. again swinging back towards a Western Front during 1943, after having repeatedly said that North Africa must act as a 'spring board' and not as a 'sofa' to future action. After urging attacks on Sardinia and Sicily he is now swinging away from there for a possible invasion of France in 1943.''

Allied pressure on Churchill

The pressure on Churchill to keep to the plan and the timetable unanimously agreed on July 27 in the previous year was not only maintained by Roosevelt, Hopkins, and Marshall in Washington, but also by Sir Archibald Clark Kerr, the British Ambassador in Moscow, who, when he was in London, informed the C.I.G.S. of the danger of going back on the decision. In his opinion, Stalin would see the postponement of the second front in the north of France as breaking a promise, and might go on to renew relations with

Hitler on the basis of a compromise. Brooke did not share the ambassador's fears. However, his suspicions were confirmed by what Kerr said; he realised that during his last interview with Stalin and Molotov, Churchill had had to make some kind of promise to Stalin, and although an engagement of this kind could not be regarded as binding, it would obviously be difficult and embarrassing for Churchill to go back on his word.

It is quite clear from the evidence that has been quoted that if there was at the time in London an influential clique of sceptical people bent on systematically rejecting any American proposals for an attack, Churchill never belonged to it; he merely accepted the unanimous discouraging opinion of his Chiefs-of-Staff with great reluctance.

We may add two further points: Churchill agreed against his will to the proposal of his Chiefs-of-Staff that the advantage the Allies were about to gain in North Africa should be exploited by moving against Sardinia, Sicily, and southern taly; secondly, he certainly never at this ime had any idea of a post-war conflict nor did he with this in mind decide to oppose Soviet or Communist expansion in the Balkans from then onwards.

Persuasive evidence can be offered for his second argument, although it arises from a later event. A few months after the Casablanca Conference, Churchill cut off all aid to General Mihailović, the Yugoslav Royalist leader, and from then on gave it exclusively to the future Marshal Tito. Moreover he had no hesitation in sending his son Randolph to Tito's headquarters as a liaison officer.

General Brooke, Admiral Sir Dudley Pound, and Air Chief-Marshal Sir Charles Portal unanimously and persistently opposed the Prime Minister's arguments in favour of Operation "Round-up" purely for strategic and technical reasons. But they might have had to accept his views if they had been strongly approved by the War Cabinet. Apparently this was not the case; in this context, Clement Attlee, who was a member of the War Cabinet as Deputy Prime Minister, Secretary of State, and Leader of the Labour Party, wrote of Churchill:

"Winston was sometimes a terrible embarrassment, for he always wanted to have a finger in every pie. But in the end after serious consideration he always accepted the verdict of the Chiefs of Staff."

But on what grounds did the Chiefs-of-Staff base the negative decision which Churchill finally accepted with much grumbling?

American military doctrine was based on the study of Napoleon's campaigns and on Jomini's works; it was corroborated by the experiences of the American Civil War (1861–65) and brought up to date in 1917 and 1918 in the light of the instruction given at the Staff College in Paris. Throughout its entire development, this doctrine was imbued with the offensive spirit. In his book *Ultra Secret* Ralph Ingersoll describes it precisely:

"Both the British Empire and the United States of America sought the complete destruction of the armed forces of the German, Japanese and Italian Empires.

"The United States of America sought this practically without qualification—that is, sought to destroy the armed forces of the enemy in the shortest possible time, by the most direct route, with only reasonable regard for risk to life and limb and no regard whatever for the expenditure of material resources. In seeking to win the war, the United States of America had no regard, either, for political considerations—it was as willing to trade with a Darlan to secure an advantage in Africa as it was to allow an advantage in the Balkans, both acts having only to pass the single test that they speeded final victory

▽ *And even from occupied Europe more reinforcements arrived to swell the armed forces of the United Nations. Here the French submarine* Casabianca, *which had managed to slip out of Toulon as the rest of the French fleet was being scuttled, is seen arriving in the North African port of Algiers.*

△ *The Presidential party en route to Casablanca. From left to right are Admiral William Leahy, Roosevelt, Harry Hopkins, and Lieutenant Howard M. Cone.*

over the armed forces of the Axis. You might sum up the American objective as: 'To destroy the armed forces of the Axis PERIOD.' "

In Ingersoll's opinion (with which we agree), British strategy was more subtle and less inclined to the offensive, at least to the offensive when both sides are strong, although the engagements at El Alamein and Caen should discourage us from making too many generalisations. On the other hand, we cannot agree with Ingersoll when he states that the British military leaders, in refusing to assume the responsibility of a second front in northern France in 1943, were influenced by considerations of international politics. Whilst the documents show that Churchill always had Allied policy in mind, it is quite clear from what has been published that Brooke, Pound, and Portal never in any way went beyond the limits of their competence and encroached on that of the Prime Minister. In fact they gave the situation at the time as their reason for recommending the postponement of the second front. At this time, the end of November 1942, the fairest thing one can say is that the future was less clear to them than to the historian, who today has the benefit of hindsight.

Thus, despite the Axis defeats at Midway, El Alamein, and Stalingrad, and the easy conquest of the North African "springboard", the situation had its dark side. In November the Allies had lost 134 ships with a gross tonnage of 807,754 tons, and Admiral Dönitz's forces continued to increase in spite of the Allied bombard-

ment of the German shipyards.

Moreover, as a result of the bad weather the slowness of the Allies, and the enemy's continual reinforcement, Operation "Torch" in Tunisia was now losing its initial surprise effect. The Allies had reckoned on occupying Cape Bon in a few days, but they were far out in their calculations.

The question was now whether to give the enemy sufficient time to fortify a strong bridgehead from Tunis to Bizerta, about 150 miles from Marsala in Sicily, whilst pretending to prepare a second front in Europe which, everyone agreed, would not in fact be launched for eight months.

On the other hand, because American troops in Great Britain and Northern Ireland had been withdrawn to join Operation "Torch", their total number had fallen to about 135,000 men at the end of the year. It was not likely that they could be brought up again to the strength of 30 divisions, including six armoured divisions, that was needed for Operation "Round-up". Brooke and Pound thought it would be impossible, in view of the U-boat threat and their lack of merchant ships. Particularly as British imports had declined in 1938–42 from 50 to 23 million tons, the United Kingdom was living on its reserves and was not capable of pursuing the war effort efficiently unless an additional supply of four million tons was obtained. With these strategic and logistic factors in mind, the British Chiefs-of-Staff concluded that in 1943 they would have to confine themselves to a moderate offensive programme. In 1946, Sir Alan Brooke read the notes he had written at the time and summarised them as follows:

"I was quite clear in my mind that the moment for the opening of a Western Front had not yet come and would not present itself during 1943. I felt we must stick to my original policy for the conduct of the war, from which I had never departed, namely, to begin with the conquest of North Africa, so as to re-open the Mediterranean, restore a million tons of shipping by avoiding Cape route; then eliminate Italy, bring in Turkey, threaten southern Europe, and then liberate France. This plan, of course, depended on Russia holding on. Although in the early stages of the war I had the most serious doubts whether she would do so, by the end of 1942 I did not think such an eventuality likely. Russia had by now withstood the attacks against Moscow, Leningrad and

Stalingrad; was getting stronger and better equipped every day. It seemed a safe bet that she would last out."

Churchill finally gave in to the arguments of his military advisers, and it must be admitted that he defended this view to Roosevelt and Hopkins as strongly as though he had never held any other.

The summit meeting that never took place

However, this change of policy appeared to require fresh consultation among all the Allies. Churchill and Roosevelt wanted Stalin to take part and the British Prime Minister suggested a meeting at Khartoum on or near January 15. Stalin, however, gave his duties as commander-in-chief as an excuse for declining the invitation from London and Washington. Undoubtedly the excuse was well justified, but nevertheless there is a significant paragraph in Stalin's reply to Churchill, which was dated December 6, 1942:

"I await a reply from you to my earlier message (of November 27, 1942) concerning the opening of a second front in western Europe in the spring of 1943."

Churchill was already completely won over to the arguments of his Chiefs-of-Staff and gave an ambiguous reply to this request:

"I am not able to reply to this question except jointly with the President of the United States. It was for this reason that I so earnestly desired a meeting between the three of us. We both understood the paramount military reasons which prevented you from leaving Russia while conducting your great operations. I am in constant communication with the President in order to see what can be done."

There is every reason to think that Stalin was not taken in by this reply. On December 14 he appealed to Roosevelt. This letter shows that General Brooke was probably right in supposing that the Prime Minister had let slip some rash remarks during his last evening in Moscow:

"Allow me also to express my confidence that time is not being lost, and that the promises about the opening of a Second

△ *Vichy French reaction to the loss of North Africa was both swift and predictable—as usual it was the Jew who was behind the Allied "theft" of France's North Africa.*

▲ Admiral Ernest J. King, Commander-in-Chief of the U.S. Fleet, which would now begin to play a more important part in Mediterranean operations, principally providing escorts and gunfire support for invasion forces.
▷ President Roosevelt reviews American armoured forces who had had their first taste of combat in the "Torch" landings.

▲ Admiral of the Fleet Sir Dudley Pound. He had been largely instrumental in bringing Britain through to the turning point in the war marked by the Casablanca Conference, but had only another nine months to live.
▷ Roosevelt meets General Henri Giraud (seated at left) on January 17, 1943. It was through Giraud that the Allies had hoped to start a rapprochement with France and so smuggled him out by submarine to North Africa.

Front in Europe given by you, Mr. President, and by Mr. Churchill in regard to 1942, and in any case in regard to the spring of 1943, will be fulfilled, and that a Second Front in Europe will be actually opened by the joint forces of Great Britain and the United States of America in the spring of next year."

But this diplomatic style shows only too clearly that Stalin's "certainty" merely expressed his lack of certainty about the matter that was worrying him so deeply. In any event, as Stalin was unable to go to Khartoum, Churchill and Roosevelt were free to choose a rendezvous closer to their respective capitals, and they settled on Anfa near Casablanca.

"Round-up" abandoned

Roosevelt travelled to Anfa in a seaplane via Belem in Brazil and Bathurst in Gambia. Harry Hopkins, his personal adviser, Admiral William D. Leahy, General Marshall, General Arnold, and Admiral King accompanied him. Churchill, who had Brooke, Pound, Portal, and Vice-Admiral Lord Louis Mountbatten, head of Combined Operations, in his party, arrived in a B-24 Liberator bomber which had been hastily adapted for passenger transport. General Sir John Dill, the British military liaison officer with the American Chiefs-of-Staff, waited for him at the Casablanca airport and had an opportunity to inform the British delegation of the prevailing atmosphere in Washington. A little later the meeting was joined by General Eisenhower, General Alexander, and Air Chief-Marshal Tedder.

The British and Americans took four days (from January 14) to reach agreement. In his memoirs, Lord Alanbrooke pays tribute to the persuasive powers of his colleagues Dill and Portal at the conference table. Churchill, too, had warmly recommended the method of "the dripping of water on a stone".

According to Sherwood, his warm admirer, Hopkins left the conference "again disappointed and depressed by the further postponement of ROUNDUP, because he was always solidly with Marshall in the conviction that there was no really adequate substitute for the opening of a Second Front in France."

Once again the C.I.G.S. was able to see Churchill privately at Casablanca, and

he has drawn the following delicious portrait of him:

"I had frequently seen him in bed, but never anything to touch the present setting. It was all I could do to remain serious. The room must have been Mrs. Taylor's bedroom and was done up in Moorish style, the ceiling was a marvellous fresco of green, blue and gold. The head of the bed rested in an alcove of Moorish design with a religious light shining on either side; the bed was covered with a light blue silk covering with 6-in wide lace *entre-deux* and the rest of the room in harmony with the Arabic ceiling. And there in the bed was Winston in his green, red and gold dragon dressing-gown, his hair, or what there was of it, standing on end, the religious lights shining on his cheeks, and a large cigar in his face! I would have given anything to have been able to take a coloured photograph of him."

In his memoirs, published in 1958, General Albert C. Wedemeyer, who was then chief of the Operations Division on General Marshall's staff, expressed his bitterness about the strategic decisions at Casablanca; even 15 years later he still felt strongly about them. According to him, Roosevelt and the American delegation had surrendered to Churchill and his astute Chiefs-of-Staff even before they had indicated to the Germans their insistence on "unconditional surrender". He wrote: "We even lost our shirts."

How can this attitude be explained? In addition to the reasons given for these Anglo-American disagreements, we should perhaps add another which has not been adequately considered. At this time the U.S.A. did not yet have enough naval forces to be a great maritime power. (Later these forces were to become superior to those of Great Britain.) In 1939 the U.S. merchant navy, including that on the Great Lakes, consisted of less than half the British and a little more than double the Norwegian tonnage: there was no reason for it to be larger, as American food supplies and industrial production did not depend on imports by sea.

Consequently the principal commanders of the American land forces were relatively insensitive to their allies' arguments concerning problems of naval logistics and transport; these had been familiar to British generals ever since the time when the "redcoats" conquered the Indies and Canada, and they therefore tended to include considerations of this problem in their strategy.

Inter-American disagreement

A further reason why the British war plans for 1943 prevailed was that they represented the unanimous views of the Prime Minister and his military advisers, whilst those on the other side of the conference table had no such consensus.

We have noted that General Marshall continued to favour the prompt opening of a second front in Europe. Admiral King expressed no opinions on the matter, but as the officer responsible for operations in the Pacific, he was susceptible to the arguments of his British colleagues in favour of Operation "Husky", whose objective was the Anglo-American capture of Sicily. The reopening of the Mediterranean from Gibraltar to Suez would save them more than a million tons of shipping, and by using a part of the tonnage released in this way they would be able to go over to a general offensive against the Japanese.

continued on page 1141

DIEPPE

Blueprint for victory - or terrible warning?

Light British naval forces head towards the beaches.
1. *A wounded survivor of the raid lies on the shingle of the Dieppe beach, waiting for medical aid.*

When the Allied war leaders met early in 1943 to draw their plans for the reconquest of Europe, the memory of the Dieppe Raid hung like a dark shadow across every scheme put forward. For on August 19, 1942, Allied troops had made their first trial of the German defences of the Atlantic coast – and they had been repulsed with appalling losses.

The basic idea which gave birth to the Dieppe Raid was to make a seaborne assault on a port within range of fighter aircraft based in southern England. The plan was to take it, hold it for a day, and pull out. There was no question of anything more ambitious. To start with, there were not enough landing-craft available to land more than about 6,000 men and (at the most optimistic maximum) 160 tanks. And the ships making up the landing force convoy would have to lie close inshore, well within range of the guns of the German defences, for over nine hours.

The operational order was clear enough: "The 2nd Canadian Division will seize JUBILEE [the codename for Dieppe] and vicinity. Occupy the area until demolition and exploitation tasks are completed. Re-embark and return to England." But "vicinity" meant an 11-mile long strip of coast with Dieppe in the centre, for the port was flanked by strong coastal batteries which would

have to be silenced to give the main assault forces a chance. This task was entrusted to Commando troops: No. 3 Commando on the left flank and No. 4 Commando on the right.

The Germans had sealed off all the natural exits from the Dieppe beaches with barbed wire and had sited machine gun positions to cover all approaches with beaten zones of fire. The shingle beach itself was like the glacis of a mediaeval castle, with a slope of 1 in 40; this rose to 1 in 10 at the sea wall, which the tanks and troops would have to negotiate before taking the town and port. Worst of all from the point of view of the attackers, however, was the fact that the Dieppe sea front had been packed with carefully camouflaged guns, making the direction of the main assault virtually impossible. Only a lightning, surprise assault across the beaches under the cover of darkness could have stood a chance – and this did not occur.

There was one flicker of success out on the right flank, where No. 4 Commando went ashore according to plan, wiped out the "Hess" battery and pulled out on schedule, before 0730 hours, having carried out its mission to the letter. But on all other sectors the attackers had run into instant disaster. On the extreme left flank the landing-craft of No. 3 Commando had got scattered during

2 *Looking inshore at the cliffs of Dieppe – a view from one of the covering destroyers.*
3. *Canadian recruiting poster. The ordeal of Dieppe was the first major operation of World War II in which Canadian troops took part.*

4. *Canadian troops in their landing craft.*
5. *The victors of Dieppe. Apart from the soundness of their defences, the Germans reacted with energy and speed to the Allied attack.*
6 *A Royal Navy motor launch (ML) with four of the landing-craft used in the Dieppe landings*

4

HAVE JUST RETURNED FROM
A DAY TRIP TO FRANCE STOP
IT WAS VERY HOT AND I DID
NOT ENJOY MYSELF STOP

Telegram by a survivor of Dieppe

The British Fairmile "C" type Motor Gun Boat

Displacement: 72 tons.
Armament: two 2-pdr and two .5-inch guns.
Speed: 26 knots.
Length: 110 feet.
Beam: 17½ feet.
Draught: 5 feet.
Complement: 16.

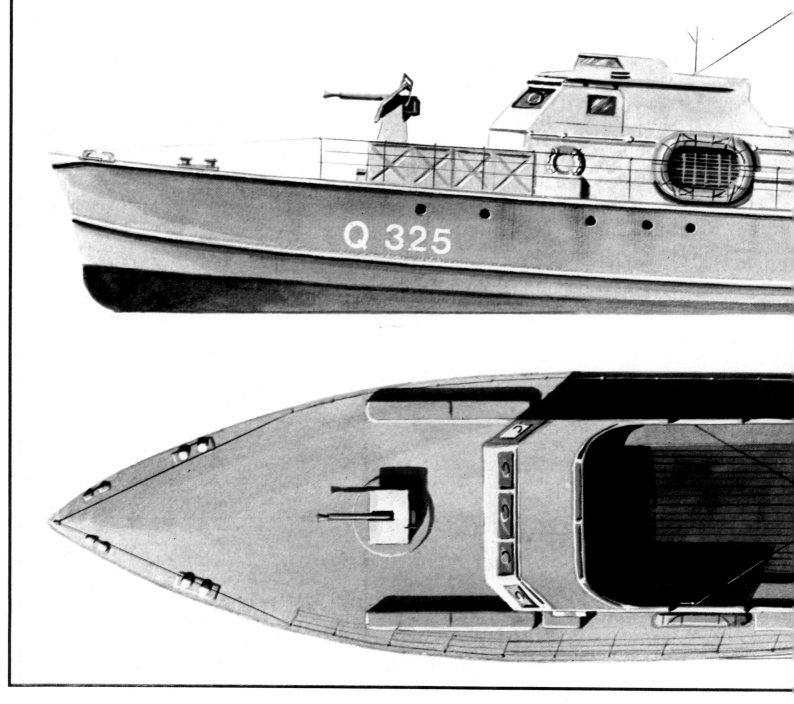

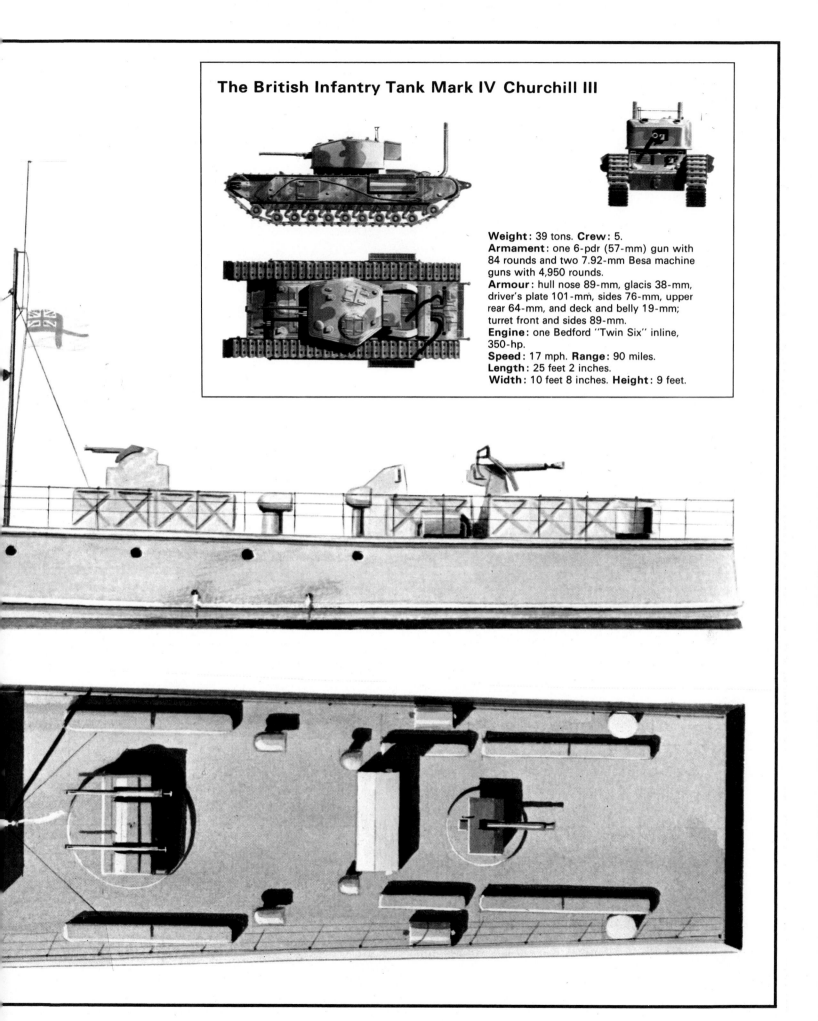

The British Infantry Tank Mark IV Churchill III

Weight: 39 tons. **Crew:** 5.
Armament: one 6-pdr (57-mm) gun with 84 rounds and two 7.92-mm Besa machine guns with 4,950 rounds.
Armour: hull nose 89-mm, glacis 38-mm, driver's plate 101-mm, sides 76-mm, upper rear 64-mm, and deck and belly 19-mm; turret front and sides 89-mm.
Engine: one Bedford "Twin Six" inline, 350-hp.
Speed: 17 mph. **Range:** 90 miles.
Length: 25 feet 2 inches.
Width: 10 feet 8 inches. **Height:** 9 feet.

7 Luftwaffe flak gunners in action in Dieppe.
8 Under the eyes of German guards, Canadian survivors give first aid to their wounded before being marched off to prison camp.
9 Symbolic of the failure of the raid: burning landing-craft and shattered tank.
10 They finally got off the beaches, but only as prisoners. The Churchill tank in the background has stripped its left-hand track in its efforts to cope with the shingle.
11 Abandoned equipment and supplies litter the floor of this burning landing-craft.

an unexpected encounter with five German armed trawlers and No. 3 Commando attacked piecemeal, many of them being pinned down on the beach under heavy cross-fire. But the worst ordeal was reserved for the Canadian forces attacking east and west of Dieppe port, on Blue, Red, White, and Green Beaches.

As the landing-craft were launched out at sea and formed up for the run-in, a muddle caused the boats carrying the Royal Regiment of Canada, destined for Blue Beach, to follow the wrong gunboat. This put them 20-odd minutes behind schedule; they landed in full daylight and were cut to pieces, only three officers and 57 men out of 27 officers and 516 men getting back to England. The Essex Scottish and Royal Hamilton Light Infantry, landing on Red and White Beaches and attacking the Dieppe sea front itself, were pinned down under the sea wall, plastered by deadly mortar fire. A few small parties and individuals, by dint of incredible courage, managed to gain the Esplanade and establish temporary footholds, but there were never enough of them to get the attack off the killing-ground of the beaches.

The intended tank support for the infantry met with similar fiasco. Only ten of the 24 tank landing-craft earmarked for the operation managed to land their tanks: a grand total of 28 tanks

12. *Curious German soldiers examine one of the abandoned landing-craft after the battle.*
13 and **14.** *Canadian prisoners and walking wounded are marched through Dieppe.*
15. *The depressing scene on Dieppe beach after the raid, showing the tanks which never even managed to get ashore. Notice the prong-shape exhaust pipe extensions to facilitate wading through shallow water.*
16. *They got home: a wounded Canadian is carried ashore from a Polish destroyer.*
17, 18, and **19.** *Survivors of the raid, safely back in England, but with the strain of the ordeal still evident on their faces.*

all of which were lost. Those that did get ashore found the heavy flint shingle extremely tough going; only three tanks managed to struggle on to the Esplanade, where they killed a few Germans, knocked down a house, and retreated to the beach with their ammunition exhausted, there to be knocked out in their turn.

Thus there was no question of sending any reinforcements, either in men or armour, to the South Saskatchewan and Queen's Own Cameron Highlanders, who had overcome the fierce German resistance on Green Beach and were closest to reaching their objectives. By 0900 hours the force commanders, Major-General Roberts and Captain Hughes-Hallett, were agreed that there was no alternative but withdrawal; and at 1022 the rescue boats began to move in to pick up the survivors. The rescue operation proved as murderous as the initial assault, but by early afternoon the battered survivors were

on their way home. At 1740 hours the War Diary of the Head quarters, German C.-in-C. West, recorded: "No armed Englishman remains on the Continent."

The cost was daunting. The Canadians lost 215 officers and 3,164 men; the Commandoes lost 24 officers and 223 men. All vehicles and equipment which had been landed were lost. Some 2,000 Canadians were taken prisoner. This amounted to a 50 per cent loss for an operation which had been a total failure. Even the test of strength in the air was a resounding defeat, the R.A.F. losing 106 aircraft for the Luftwaffe's 48 destroyed and 24 damaged.

The reasons were insufficient information, bad communications, and a plan calling for total surprise over a wide front. The lessons: the need for total air superiority, tighter control over the forming-up of the landing-craft, and the need to land sufficient armour to shield the attacking infantry.

△ *German comment on the Allied discussions in North Africa had an element of truth about it, but not to the extent claimed here, with peevish Allied leaders not wishing to sit at the same table.*
▷ *The "big two" meet on the lawn of Roosevelt's villa at Casablanca.*
▽ *American protagonists at Casablanca. Left to right seated: Marshall, Roosevelt, and King; standing: Hopkins, Lieutenant-General "Hap" Arnold, Lieutenant-General Brehon Somervell, and Averell Harriman.*

ontinued from page 1129

For different reasons, General H. H. Arnold of the U.S. Army Air Forces came to similar conclusions, for he maintained the view that the aerial bombardment alone of the German industrial centres would drive the Third Reich to defeat. To achieve this purpose Arnold favoured first eliminating Italy from the war. This would enable him to station a powerful force of strategic bombers in the Foggia area, to crush the objectives which had previously been out of range of the squadrons based on British and North African airfields.

It is quite possible that the idea of following up Operation "Husky" with a landing in southern Italy (Operation "Avalanche") came about in this indirect way, without anyone being aware of it.

It is now clear that General Marshall's opinion did not prevail at the conclusion of the sometimes lively debates of the Combined Chiefs-of-Staff Committee. In fact, in the list of recommendations submitted by the committee on January 23 for the approval of the U.S. President and the British Prime Minister, "Operations from the United Kingdom" took only fourth place among those for 1943.

Security of sea communications had absolute priority, which is not surprising, as without them there would have been no need to consider any other aims. Then came military and economic assistance to the Soviet Union; then the Mediterranean operations, for which General Alexander was assigned to General Eisenhower as deputy commander; as part of these, it was planned to launch "Husky" at the time of the full moon in July.

Only after these recommendations did the documents compiled by the Chiefs-of-Staff include a section on the operations they proposed to launch from Great Britain. These are summarised as follows by Churchill in his memoirs:

"The heaviest possible air offensive against German war effort.

"Such limited offensive operations as may be practicable with the amphibious forces available.

"The assembly of the strongest possible force in constant readiness to re-enter the Continent as soon as German resistance is weakened to the required extent."

It is clear that the possibility of opening a second front in France was conditional on a state of affairs existing in 1943 which would be extremely problematical, to say the least. It was most unlikely that the German forces on the continent would be "sufficiently weakened" by August 1 for

such an operation to be authorised.

In the Pacific and the Far East, the two Allied powers would go on applying continuous pressure on Japan, but their operations, according to the recommendations to the President and the Prime Minister, "must be kept within such limits as will not, in the opinion of the Joint Chiefs of Staff, jeopardise the capacity of the United Nations to take advantage of any favourable opportunity for the decisive defeat of Germany in 1943."

With this reservation, Nimitz was authorised to assign the Caroline and the Marshall Islands as an objective to the American air and naval forces in the Pacific. At the same time, the British C.-in-C. in the Far East would prepare and launch Operation "Anakim", with the object of expelling the Japanese from Burma. The Allies would therefore gain starting positions from which to destroy the Japanese Empire as soon as the Third Reich was defeated.

Lastly it was agreed that Britain alone would be responsible for relations with Turkey; it was therefore her duty to take measures to bring the Ankara Government within the field of the United Nations and into active participation in the war against Germany and Italy.

△ △ *Seeing themselves as rivals for the leadership of the French serving with the Allies, Giraud and de Gaulle did not at first see eye to eye–de Gaulle even refused to go to Casablanca at first, only arriving on January 22.*

△ *An all-too-accurate German assessment of the rapprochement between Giraud and de Gaulle. Overleaf: A study in contrasts at Casablanca. From left to right an indifferent Giraud, neutral Roosevelt, bored de Gaulle, and happy Churchill.*

"Unconditional surrender"

This was the programme for the conduct of the war in 1943 which was formulated at Casablanca by the Combined Chiefs-of-Staff Committee. There was nothing particularly impressive about it, it was true, and without actually saying so, it postponed the final decision till 1944. It must be admitted, however, that it satisfied the basic principle of all strategy, that of apportioning one's objectives according to the means at one's disposal.

There followed the famous press conference of January 24, 1943, in the course of which Roosevelt declared that the two Anglo-Saxon powers could reduce their war aims to "the simple formula of placing the objective of this war in terms of an unconditional surrender by Germany, Italy and Japan."

Ever since this occasion there have been many different interpretations by both sides about this declaration, its background, and its consequences; we are not able to give a comprehensive account of them here and shall therefore merely give a small selection of evidence which, however, is of great importance, beginning with Roosevelt's. According to his account, the part of the Casablanca declaration referred to was not agreed with Churchill; he had blurted out the words entirely by chance. Before they received the press on the Sunday January 24, the two statesmen had presided at the reconciliation between Generals Giraud and de Gaulle and Roosevelt commented:

"We had so much trouble getting those two French generals together that I thought to myself that this was as difficult as arranging the meeting of Grant and Lee—and then suddenly the Press conference was on, and Winston and I had had no time to prepare for it, and the thought popped into my mind that they had called Grant 'Old Unconditional Surrender' and the next thing I knew I had said it."

Roosevelt's explanation therefore is that he was rather pressed and that he was reminded of the American Civil War and the nickname "Unconditional Surrender" given by the Union troops to General Ulysses S. Grant. This explanation appears unconvincing to us; Hopkins' biographer R. E. Sherwood has in fact included photographs of the conference in his book and these show the President with a sheaf of papers in his hand.

Did Churchill give his consent?

Churchill in his memoirs admits that when he replied to Ernest Bevin, Foreign Secretary in the Labour Government, on July 11, 1949, he gave a sincere but inaccurate version of this incident when he said he had never heard the words "unconditional surrender" until they escaped from the President's lips on January 24, 1943. Churchill's sincerity is unquestionable; the evidence he has produced is invaluable in establishing the facts of the situation.

On January 20 he wrote a long report on the way the conference was progressing for Clement Attlee and the War Cabinet.

The sixth of Churchill's eight paragraphs reads:

"We propose to draw up a statement of the work of the conference for communication to the Press at the proper time. I should be glad to know what the War Cabinet would think of our including in this statement a declaration of the firm intention of the United States and the British Empire to continue the war relentlessly until we have brought about the 'unconditional surrender' of Germany and Japan. The omission of Italy would be to encourage a break-up there. The President liked this idea, and it would stimulate our friends in every country."

The War Cabinet met immediately and replied to the Prime Minister's question by return of post in the negative; the message giving their views left London on January 21:

its application to Germany and Japan;
3. the War Cabinet, which was duly consulted, raised no objections to the proposed formula, but accepted it unanimously; and
4. in particular its chairman, Clement Attlee, the deputy Prime Minister, and Ernest Bevin, the Minister of Employment and National Service, were completely wrong in trying to disown the responsibilities they had undertaken at the time.

Doubtless the former Prime Minister was particularly concerned with this last point after the altercation on July 11, 1949.

However, it must be admitted that by Churchill's account, the final communiqué summarising the work of the conference for the press, in the version agreed with the American President, contained no mention of "unconditional surrender". Churchill was therefore extremely surprised on January 24 to hear his powerful ally and friend proclaim this radical programme to the listening world. But again, when one compares the versions of the two protagonists in this tragi-comedy, one must perhaps admit that they are less contradictory than appears at first; at least this is so if one agrees that Roosevelt's proved blunder consisted in disclosing a formula which had received Churchill's complete agreement, but which the latter would have preferred to keep a secret.

The question arises whether the Casablanca statements resulted in prolonging and intensifying the war. Did it, in short, play the dictators' game by uniting their peoples and their armies behind them? Just at this time the first signs of disunity were becoming apparent, and these could perhaps have been exploited if the nations had been told that their fate would not be so grievous if they got rid of Hitler, Tojo, and Mussolini by their own efforts.

Churchill denied that the statement played into the dictators' hands, in spite, as he said, of the views to the contrary of a whole school of thought both in England and in America. We must state frankly that we cannot agree with him. Moreover, we must point out that on three occasions the Prime Minister felt impelled to return to the subject and spell out to the entire world what the phrase "unconditional surrender" did and did not mean, at the Guildhall on June 30, 1943, and in the House of Commons on February 22, 1944 and January 18, 1945. It is unlikely that he would have done this if in the meantime

General Sir Alan Brooke was born in 1883 and entered the Army via Woolwich Academy. As commander of II Corps in 1940, Brooke fought a masterly rearguard action covering the retreat to Dunkirk, and was later that year appointed C.-in-C. Home Forces, with the immensely difficult task of organising the defences against the expected German invasion. Brooke succeeded Sir John Dill as Chief of the Imperial General Staff late in 1941, and became Chairman of the Chiefs-of-Staff Committee in June 1942. In this capacity he was at the head of the military establishment in Great Britain, with the difficult problem of translating the ideas dreamed up by Churchill into realistic terms, and dissuading their author from those that were impossible.

"The Cabinet were unanimously of opinion that balance of advantage lay against excluding Italy, because of misgivings which would inevitably be caused in Turkey, in the Balkans, and elsewhere. Nor are we convinced that effect on Italians would be good. Knowledge of all rough stuff coming to them is surely more likely to have desired effect on Italian morale."

Whatever opinion may be held of the validity of these arguments, the documents quoted by Churchill, whose authenticity has never been challenged, clearly show, with regard to the formula "unconditional surrender", that
1. it was the result of an Anglo-American agreement on January 20, 1943 or previously;
2. the British Prime Minister freely gave it his complete support, at least in

it had not become apparent to him that the Casablanca statement had been very much grist to the National-Socialist propaganda mill.

President Roosevelt was in a similar position. Admittedly Robert Sherwood is right in claiming that the Casablanca statement somewhat reassured a section of the American public which had been brought close to hysteria by the agreement between Eisenhower and Darlan; this section now realised that there would be no negotiations either with Göring in Germany or Matsuoka in Japan. Nevertheless, in doing this, the White House and Harry Hopkins never actually dissociated themselves from a viewpoint favouring negotiations.

Many centuries ago, the Chinese general Sun Tsu, the author of the first treatise on war in history, was shrewder; in fact he advised his readers not to inflict a uniformly severe treatment on their prisoners-of-war. For, he wrote with admirable good sense, if you behead all your prisoners, "no-one will ever give himself up".

Amongst the Germans, the general tendency has been to agree with the arguments of the British and American critics

of Churchill and Roosevelt. To take just one example, Colonel-General Guderian writes as follows:

"For us the most important result of this conference was the insistence that the Axis Powers surrender unconditionally. The effect of this brutal formula on the German nation and, above all, on the Army was great. The soldiers, at least, were convinced from now on that our enemies had decided on the utter destruction of Germany, that they were no longer fighting – as Allied propaganda at the time alleged – against Hitler and so-called Nazism, but against their efficient, and therefore dangerous, rivals for the trade of the world."

Although Guderian, who was without any doubt a great general, here shows somewhat doubtful judgement, the Casablanca declaration clearly dealt a hard blow at the anti-Hitler opposition in Germany. In fact it did not discourage the group organised around Dr. Goerdeler, the former Mayor of Leipzig; this group included Colonel-General Beck, the former Chief-of-Staff of the Army, Colonel-General Hoeppner, relieved of his command of the 4th *Panzerarmee* by Hitler for disobeying an order, and Field-Marshal von Witzleben. However, the declaration closed many doors; for instance Field-Marshals Rommel, von Manstein, von Rundstedt, and Guderian himself refused to listen to the group. Guderian, recalling a visit at the time from Goerdeler, wrote in 1950:

"The weaknesses and mistakes of the National-Socialist system and the personal errors that Hitler made were by then plain to see–even to me; attempts must therefore be made to remedy them. In view of Germany's dangerous situation as a result of the Stalingrad catastrophe and of the demands made for unconditional surrender to all its enemies (including the Soviet Union) a way would have to be found that did not lead to a disaster for the country and the people. Hence the vast responsibility and the enormous difficulties that confronted anyone who tried to think quietly how we might best hope still to save Germany."

This significant passage shows that the members of the officer corps in the main felt no hatred or scorn for the English and the Americans. But they dreaded a national catastrophe if the Soviet Union, of whose terrible power they had gained experience, was included, as Roosevelt and Churchill intended, in the Casablanca statement. The least one can say is that events did not prove them wrong.

Franco's conclusions

General Franco was equally perceptive. On the following February 21, when he considered the consequences of the Casablanca decisions and the battle of Stalingrad, he wrote the following prophetic lines to Sir Samuel Hoare, the British Ambassador in Madrid:

"If events develop in the future as they have up to now, it would be Russia which would penetrate deeply into German territory. And we ask the question: if this should occur, which is the greater danger not only for the Continent, but for England herself, a Germany not totally defeated but with sufficient strength to serve as a rampart against Communism, a Germany hated by all her neighbours, which would deprive her of all authority though she remained intact, or a Sovietized Germany which would certainly furnish Russia with the added strength of her war preparations, her engineers, her specialised workmen and technicians, which would enable Russia to extend herself with an empire without precedent from the Atlantic to the Pacific? . . .

"And we ask a second question: is there anybody in the centre of Europe, in that mosaic of countries without consistency or unity, bled moreover by war and foreign domination, who could contain the ambitions of Stalin? There is certainly no one . . . We may be sure that after the German domination, the only domination which could live in the countries is Communism. For this reason we consider the situation is extremely grave and think that people in England should reflect calmly on the matter, since should Russia succeed in conquering Germany, there will be no one who can contain her . . .

"If Germany had not existed Europeans would have invented her and it would be ridiculous to think that her place could be taken by a confederation of Lithuanians, Poles, Czechs and Rumanians which would rapidly be converted into so many more states of the Soviet confederation."

It is likely, but it has not been confirmed, that Sir Samuel Hoare passed General Franco's warning on to the British Government. When he replied on February 25, he must have been sure that

▽ *General Arnold and Air Chief-Marshal Sir Charles Portal (right), the Chief of the Air Staff, in conversation at Casablanca. Portal was strongly in favour of more Mediterranean enterprises, as they would prevent the Germans from moving forces to Russia or the Channel coast.*

neither Downing Street nor the Foreign Office would dissociate themselves from what he wrote. There appears to be a certain sense of superiority, as well as robust good sense, in his words:

"Will any single country be able to dominate Europe at the end of this war? Russia, at least will need a long period of reconstruction and recovery in which she

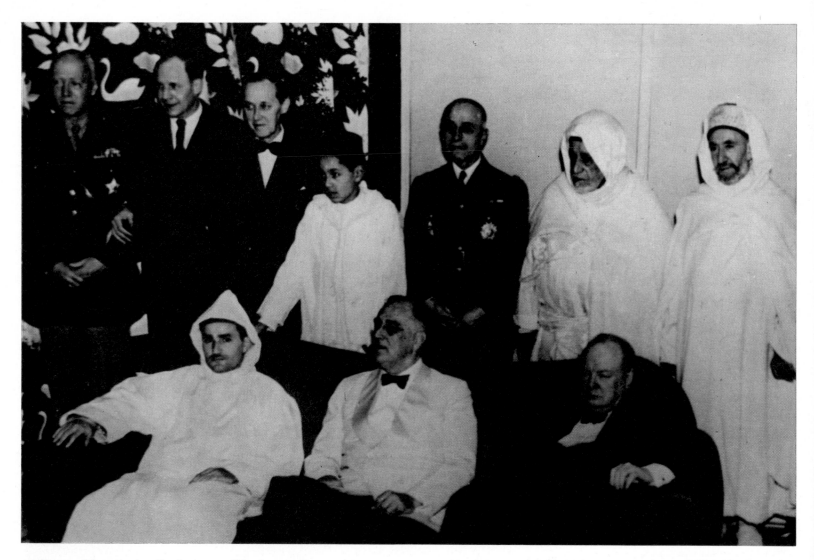

△ Roosevelt's reception for the Sultan Mohammed V of Morocco (on Roosevelt's right). Behind the Sultan is Crown Prince Hassan, with General Noguès, the Resident-General of Morocco, on his left.

will depend greatly upon the British Empire and the United States of America for economic help . . . There will then (after the war) undoubtedly be great British and American armies on the Continent . . . They will be composed of fresh, front-line troops, whose ranks will not have been previously decimated by years of exhausting war on the Russian front . . .

"As for ourselves, I make the confident prophecy that at that moment Great Britain will be the strongest European power . . . British influence, it seems to me, will be stronger in Europe than at any time since the fall of Napoleon.

". . . We shall not shirk our responsibilities to European civilisation or throw away our great strength by premature unilateral disarmament. Having, with our Allies, won the war, we intend to maintain our full influence in Europe, and to take our full share in its reconstruction."

"Above war, there is peace," said Marshal Foch in 1918. By this he meant that victory is not an end in itself, but that it must give the victor an advan-

tageous position in a new balance of political powers. Britain had succeeded perfectly in doing this at the Treaty of Utrecht in 1713 and the Congress of Vienna in 1815. She thought it was her task to do it at Versailles in 1919, when she took up the German case against her French ally. Possibly Churchill adopted the attitude we have described because he was mindful of this error, and he maintained it until the Teheran conference.

Just as every individual and collective human tragedy has its funny side, we may imagine how President Roosevelt would have felt if after the sumptuous reception he gave for the Sultan of Morocco Mohammed V, he had found out that his Sherifian Majesty, after receiving reports from his trusty *caids*, gave the information to the German consul-general at Tangier. When we examine this incident years later, we can pay tribute to the memory of the late Sultan, who though he was not able to penetrate the great secrets of the conduct of the war, performed his mission as the *Abwehr*'s minor agent with diligence and conscientiousness.

CHAPTER 83
American build-up

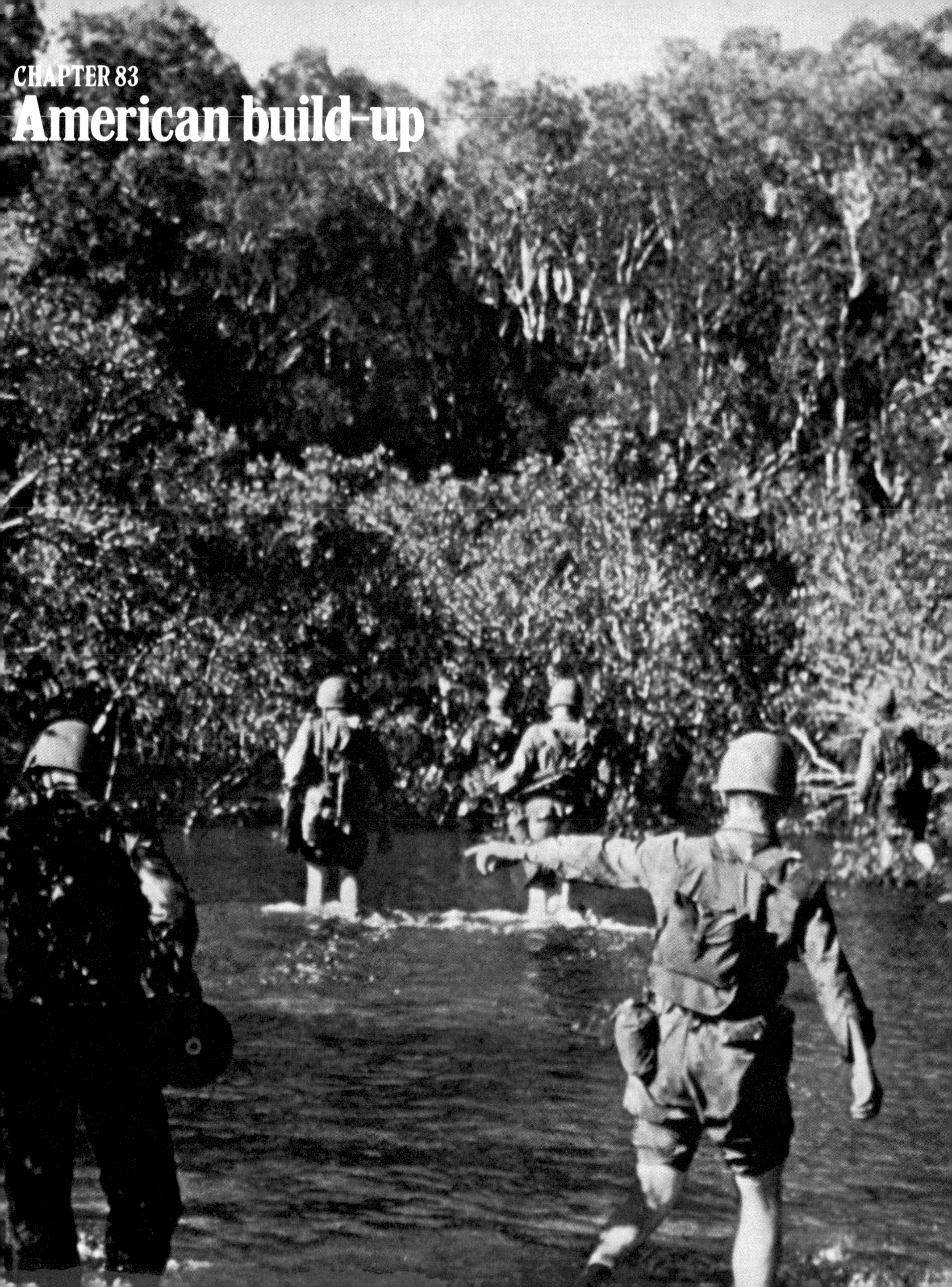

The year 1943 was to see the young army of the United States engaged successively in Tunisia, in Sicily, and then in southern Italy; hence it is important for the reader to know its most original features.

On the day that World War II began, September 1, 1939, the American land forces were as unprepared in terms of men and *matériel* as they had been in August 1914. Six years later, on September 2, 1945, the day that Shigemitsu, the Japanese Prime Minister, and General Umezu, Chief of the Imperial General Staff, signed the terms of surrender for the Japanese Empire, they had put into service four army groups, nine armies, 23 corps, 89 divisions (including 67 infantry, one cavalry, 16 armoured, and five airborne). These were supported, covered, and moved by 12 air forces totalling 273 air combat groups which, on the day of the surrender of the Japanese Empire, were divided into five very heavy bomber, 96 heavy bomber, 26 medium bomber, 8 light bomber, 87 fighter, 24 reconnaissance, and 27 transport groups.

On the same day, the United States Army had 7,700,000 officers, N.C.O.s, and other ranks, including 100,000 W.A.C.s (Women's Army Corps), serving under the colours. It counted for just over half of the 14 million young Americans who were, in one respect or another, affected by the general mobilisation order which was the response to the attack on Pearl Harbor.

Compared with the 17 million Germans who donned one of the several uniforms of the Wehrmacht or of the *Waffen* S.S., out of a total population of between 80 and 90 millions, the figure of 14 million Americans seems insignificant. Likewise in comparison with the 22 million men and women whom the Soviet Union hurled into the heat of the conflict between June 22, 1941 and September 15, 1945.

But these comparisons are only part of the truth. It will be remembered that on September 1, 1939 Hitler had at his disposal 108 fully trained, officered, and equipped divisions, and that on June 22, 1941 Stalin was able to call on at least 178 to face the German aggressor alone, whereas when the war began in Europe, the Regular Army of the United States comprised only five divisions, numbering abour 188,500 men and 14,400 officers. Hence everything (in every sphere – recruitment, training, equipment) had to be built up from this minute nucleus.

The burden of Lend-Lease

Furthermore, we must not forget that the "great arsenal of democracy" was not exclusively at the service of the American armed forces. By virtue of the Lend-Lease Act, war material had to be supplied to powers allied to the United States. According to the final two-yearly report addressed to the Secretary of State for War on September 1, 1945, military equipment worth more than 20,000 million dollars was made over to Great Britain, the Soviet Union, China, France, etc., enough, it assures us, to equip fully no fewer than 2,000 infantry or 588 armoured divisions. These Lend-Lease supplies could only act as a brake and restriction on the American armed forces, both in view of the personnel required in their manufacture and transport overseas, and because of the delays consequently imposed on the organisation and training of units.

Mention has already been made of the irritation felt by General MacArthur at the thought of all the *matériel* President Roosevelt was sending to the Soviet Union, when he was left virtually destitute in the Philippines; one might also allude to the case of the armoured division stripped of the 300 Sherman tanks it had only recently received, so as to re-equip the British 8th Army, which had lost most of its tanks in the heavy fighting between Bir Hakeim and Tobruk. But what alternative was there? None it seems, judging by the fact that, in the main, General Marshall, Army Chief-of-Staff and Chairman of the Joint Chiefs-of-Staff Committee, never on this issue came into conflict with Franklin Roosevelt or Harry Hopkins.

Marshall's superb performance

Taking into account all the constraints that stood in the way of the natural growth of the American land forces, one is all the more astounded at the tremendous effort made and the impressive results achieved between 1939 and 1944.

Credit for this is due to General of the Army George Catlett Marshall, whom President Roosevelt, so discerning in the choice of men so long as political con-

Page 1149: Men of the 41st Infantry Division wade through a swamp after making a practice assault landing in Australia.

◁△ *West Point cadets at grenade practice. On these early classes of the war would devolve much of the junior leadership of the expanding American Army.*
◁▽ *U.S. "Seabees" scramble over an obstacle on an assault course. The Seabees, U.S. Navy construction engineers, won a great name for themselves in construction work under the most arduous and hostile conditions in the Pacific.*
▽ *Officer candidates at similar work at a U.S. Army training camp in England. Many of these would be senior N.C.O.s.*

War Bonds
ARE CHEAPER THAN WOODEN CROSSES

siderations were not involved, had called to the post of Chief of the General Staff on September 1, 1939.

In the words of Sir John Dill, head of the British military delegation in Washington, writing to the Chief of the Imperial General Staff at the end of March 1942, he was "a man who improved immensely on acquaintance—straight, clear-headed, and loved by all: not a strategist, full of character and humour."

Lord Alanbrooke wrote as follows about his American colleague in 1946:

"There was a great charm and dignity about Marshall which could not fail to appeal to one; a big man and a very great gentleman who inspired trust but did not impress me by the ability of his brain."

We shall let Field-Marshals Dill and Alanbrooke bear the responsibility for their judgement as to Marshall's shortcomings as a strategist, which have all the appearance of being attributable to a quite divergent conception of the general conduct of operations, but the testimony of Sir Arthur Bryant is of value here the better to point the characteristics of the man he calls the "great Virginian":

"Without the great Virginian's strength of purpose and administrative ability the

American armies could never have been made so swiftly the instrument of victory they became. Between Pearl Harbor and D-Day Marshall did for America, and on a far vaster scale, what Carnot did for Revolutionary France and Kitchener for Britain."

Yet an army, be it large or small, is something other than an administrative or

△ △ *American mountain troops in training for the day when Europe would be invaded.*
△ *Meal break for U.S. troops training in Australia.*

1153

△ *Part of the first batch of 650 W.A.A.C.s to arrive in Great Britain marches into an 8th Air Force base. The steadily growing number of W.A.A.C.s allowed men to be withdrawn from clerical duties and the like for more active service.*

▽ *America was able to provide most of her own raw materials for the war production programme, but natural resources had to be conserved so that expansion could continue in the future.*

organisational entity. It is also a pyramidic structure of human beings, most of them attached to the military concept of duty, all of them subject to the rigours of military discipline, whence the primary importance attaching to officer selection, to every aspect of officer training, and to appointments to high command.

In this respect, it has sometimes been unrecognised outside America that military staff training in the United States had been revolutionised as a result of the 1918 campaign, when the inadequacy of the rear area troops so contrasted with the *élan* of the front-line troops. There is no question at all that the Infantry School at Fort Benning and the Command and General Staff School at Fort Leavensworth were quite comparable with similar institutions in France, Germany, and Great Britain.

Nevertheless, although military leaders are never found among those who fail to pass out of staff college, the cream of any one year are not all military leaders; so of necessity there is a final stage in promotion, the most vital of all, and one is bound to recognise that Marshall's discernment here was unequalled. A close examination

of the orders of battle of the different belligerents in World War II provides evidence that, in relation to other armies, American generals relieved of their command during active service were relatively few, thus vindicating Marshall's appointments.

And yet the task before him was a gigantic one, in order to move from a small professional army of five divisions to a great national army numbering 89, without the quality suffering from such a rapid rate of increase. One example will suffice to justify this statement: an example taken from the memoirs of General of the Army Omar Nelson Bradley, who is here describing the difficulties of every kind that he encountered during 1942, in the organisation and training of the 28th Infantry Division:

"The 28th Division was then undergoing the troubles that plagued so many National Guard divisions during mobilisation. Like others called into federal service in 1940 and 1941, the 28th Division had been cannibalized again and again for cadres in formation of new divisions. In addition, hundreds of its finest non-commissioned officers had been sent to officer training schools. Many more of its

The U.S. 105-mm Howitzer Motor Carriage M7B1

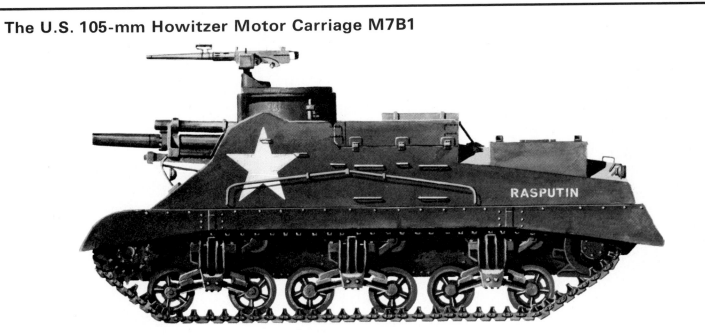

Weight: 22½ tons.
Crew: 7.
Armament: one 105-mm M1A2, M2, or M2A1 howitzer with 69 rounds and one .5-inch Browning machine gun with 300 rounds.
Armour: 62-mm maximum, 12-mm minimum.
Engine: one Ford GAA inline, 450-hp.
Speed: 26 mph.
Range: 125 miles.
Length: 20 feet 3¾ inches.
Width: 9 feet 5¼ inches.
Height: 8 feet 4 inches.

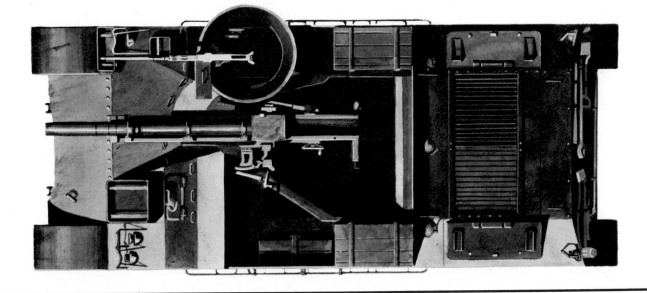

▷ *Willys Jeeps in two of their many roles: with rocket launching gear (foreground) and in its more common guise as a liaison and reconnaissance vehicle. A total of 639,245 "jeeps" of various kinds was built during the war years.*
▷ ▷ *U.S. troops in the Pacific.*

best-qualified men transferred to the air corps as flying cadets. These vacancies in the divisions were then filled with periodic transfusions of draftees, leaving the division in a constant state of unpreparedness. In June, 1942, I was ordered from the 82nd to take command of the 28th, whip those unbalanced units into a trim division, and ready it for the field.

"For months afterwards the 28th Division continued to be bled both for cadres and officer candidate quotas. The constant turnover in personnel gutted our progress in training, and throughout the entire division we became desperately short of junior officers and noncoms. Only too often companies were commanded by second lieutenants assisted by sergeants.

"Finally when IV Corps called for still another cadre to form a new division, I said, 'Fine, we'll send you one. But then suppose you send us a cadre so we can get along here.'"

Lord Alanbrooke, as we have seen, describes General Marshall as a "very great gentleman". Let this be the final touch to his portrait. And indeed a man who was able to live on good terms with a colleague as awkward as Admiral King and command the respect of a subordinate as difficult as General MacArthur, must have been distinguished by outstanding qualities of balanced leadership, tact, evenness of temper and shining integrity. Furthermore, in his capacity as chairman of the Joint Chiefs-of-Staff, which constituted a sort of link between the military command and the government, he enjoyed the entire confidence of Secretary of War Henry Stimson and of President Roosevelt. In addition to this, he was held in esteem by, and had ready access to, the Senate, which was not unimportant in view of the Senate's watching brief on the appointment of general officers.

American military organisation

Let us now attempt to describe the larger military formations of the American army, with emphasis less on what they had in common with, than on what distinguished them from the formations we have already encountered. In both the Red Army and the Wehrmacht, as we have seen, the basic tank or armoured formation altered from the brigade or division to the corps or army (between 1939 and 1941 in the case of the Germans, 1940 and 1942 for the Russians). There was no such development with the Americans, where the norm remained the division. Was this a defect of organisation, as has been suggested?

Infantry and armour

The American infantry division was completely motorised, numbering 1,440 vehicles for 14,253 officers, N.C.O.s, and other ranks. Hence in attack it was possible within a corps to couple armoured and infantry formations without their disintegrating once they started moving, as occurred on so many occasions on the Eastern Front, where infantry or horse-drawn units found it hard going to keep up with advancing mechanised units. Thus of 328 German divisions that had been or were being formed on October 4, 1943, there were no more than 46 that could be considered as armoured or motorised. It is

nevertheless true that if wholly motorised units proved their worth in the plains of France and Germany, they were to give plenty of trouble to the Americans in the mountainous regions of southern Italy, where communications were poor. During the winter of 1943/4, the American 5th Army, incapable of manoeuvring across the mountains, was reduced–with the negative results that are common knowledge–to pounding away at the fortress of Cassino.

Taken altogether, with its three infantry regiments (nine battalions), artillery regiment consisting of four groups each of 12 howitzers (three of 105-mm and one of 155-mm weapons), engineer battalion, signals company, medical battalion, and supply and maintenance units, the American infantry division was in no essential way different from its European and Japanese counterparts.

On the other hand, it is quite another story with the armoured division in the form given it at Fort Knox (the American "tankodrome") by General Chaffee, with the influential support of General Marshall; it was Chaffee who in the

United States played the rôle of Colonel de Gaulle and General Guderian.

Its order of battle consisted of a reconnaissance battalion, four battalions of medium tanks, three battalions of infantry in half-tracks, three battalions of self-propelled 105-mm howitzers (18 in each), an engineer battalion, a separate engineer company, a medical battalion, a repair and maintenance battalion, and other rear formations. The whole comprised, in its 1942 form, 159 medium M4 Sherman type tanks, 68 light M3 Stuart tanks, 68 8-ton armoured cars, and rather more than 1,100 wheeled all-purpose vehicles for the division's 651 officers and 10,248 N.C.O.s and other ranks.

Compared with the Panzer division in its 1943 form, the American armoured division had 227 tanks as against 160. Its three infantry battalions moved up into the combat zone in lightly armoured half-tracks, whereas the Germans were only able to mechanise one battalion in every four. With artillery the picture is the same. The Americans equipped the three artillery battalions with self-propelled guns based on Sherman chassis, whereas the Panzer division had only one of its artillery regiments equipped with self-propelled guns.

But above all, the originality of the American armoured divisions lay in the fact that they were flexibly assembled in tactical groups whose composition was fixed; known as Combat Commands, these incorporated at regimental level one tank battalion (17 Stuart and 51 Sherman tanks), one battalion of motorised infantry, and a battalion of self-propelled howitzers, under a single commander supported by a staff. An armoured division had two combat commands, the rest of the division's forces forming the commander's reserve. This system of organisation, which simplified the exercise of command by decentralising it, produced such good results that for the 1944 campaign it was decided to organise a third combat command in each division.

Finally, it should be said that unlike parallel European units, the American division had neither an anti-tank nor an anti-aircraft detachment as part of its equipment. These were allocated on a temporary basis from a higher échelon as the situation demanded; even so, every Sherman tank and every self-propelled howitzer was armed with a .5-inch anti-aircraft machine gun, quite sufficient to hold off low-flying aircraft.

◁△ *The "Bazooka", with the crew's No. 2 loading a round. The calibre was 2.36 inches, length 54 inches, and weight 12 pounds. Maximum effective range was about 400 yards.*
◁▽ *A German Pzkw IV medium tank captured in North Africa is lowered down to the quayside in an American port. From here it was to be shipped to the Aberdeen Proving Grounds in Maryland for examination and testing. The results were invaluable in the design of counter-weapons, such as the bazooka above and anti-tank artillery.*
▽ *General Adna R. Chaffee, the father of American armoured strength.*

I need you on the job *full time*...
DON'T GET HURT

New *matériel*

The American Army faced the test of battle with equipment that was wholly new and, with very few exceptions, well suited to combat conditions – strong and sturdy, easy to learn to handle and to maintain, and designed for mass-production: for instance the Jeep and the Walkie-Talkie radio.

Certainly the standard American army tank, the M4 Sherman, even with its 75-mm (40 calibre) exchanged for a British-made 76.2-mm (58 calibre) gun, was no match for German machines of the same year of manufacture. But it must be remembered that if it had had to be prematurely discarded in favour of a more powerful, hence heavier machine, the transportation plans for Operation "Round-up", subsequently "Overlord", would have required total revision, and this would have involved discarding several hundred landing craft which had been built around the Sherman's specifications.

General Marshall, replying to certain criticisms, vindicated his action here in seemingly irrefutable terms:

"Our tanks had to be shipped thousands of miles overseas and landed on hostile shores amphibiously. They had to be able to cross innumerable rivers on temporary bridges, since when we attacked we sought to destroy the permanent bridges behind the enemy lines from the air. Those that our planes missed were destroyed by the enemy when he retreated. Therefore our tanks could not well be of the heavy type. We designed our armour as a weapon of exploitation. In other words we desired to use our tanks in long range thrusts deep into the enemy's rear where they could chew his supply installations and communications. This required great endurance – low consumption of gasoline and ability to move great distances without break-down.

"But while that was the most profitable use of the tank, it became unavoidable in stagnant prepared-line fighting to escape tank-to-tank battles. In this combat, our medium tank was at a disadvantage, when forced into head-on engagement with the German heavies."

A new type of anti-tank weapon

In the face of the enemy's tanks, the American infantryman possessed a weapon that was both sturdy and ingenious. The "bazooka" got its name from a musical instrument then popular in the United States. Its punch was the result of using a hollow charge warhead, whose effect on armour-plating was well known, before the war, to ordnance experts in both continents. On May 10, 1940 the Germans tried it out for the first time when they detonated charges of this type against the casemates of Fort Eben-Emaël. At the same time, a grenade-firing rifle, working on the same principle, had been ordered as a standard weapon by the French Army, and indeed had its production been accelerated there is no doubt that the Panzer divisions would not have found it so easy to cross the Meuse.

However, the file concerning this invention, which originated in Switzerland, was transferred to Washington by Vichy, in addition to that of the B1 *bis* tank. Then an American inventor had the idea of fitting a rocket-launcher to the base of the hollow charge grenade and of firing it through an open ended tube. The weapon's range was up to 400 yards, which left the infantryman only 30 seconds to take aim, but it was capable of penetrating five inches of armour plate and, if the right circumstances presented themselves, of blowing up the tank's supply of petrol and ammunition.

Evidence of their destructive power was to be seen after the war, for example in Normandy and Alsace where the wrecks of armoured vehicles were still strewn across the 1944 and 1945 battlefields.

In the infantry regiments, the M3 37-mm anti-tank gun had to be replaced almost on the spur of the moment by the British 57-mm 6-pounder, which had come into service, with highly successful results, on the El Alamein front during the previous summer. But at army and corps level, there were still anti-tank battalions equipped with the M5 75-mm gun firing a 12½-lb armour-piercing shell at a muzzle velocity of 2,800 feet per second. Initially it was fitted onto half-tracks, but the results were so discouraging that the weapon acquired the name of Purple Heart Box after the American medal for wounds received in action. It was quickly abandoned in favour of a device given the

◁△ U.S. combat engineers prepare to tow off a "knocked out" Stuart light tank during an exercise in southern England. ◁▽ A lesson that hardly needed bringing home to combat troops. ▽ The U.S. M3 37-mm anti-tank gun. This gun, which fired a 1.6-pound projectile, was the standard American anti-tank gun at the beginning of the war, but was no better than the already obsolete British 2-pdr. It was soon replaced by the M1 57-mm gun firing a 6.3-pound projectile.

designation number M10; mounted in an open turret on a Sherman chassis, it was completely satisfactory.

It has been alleged, sometimes in print, that the United States Army was too lavishly equipped and that its rear formations operated on a gigantic scale. They certainly contained laundering companies and shower units, naturally enough motorised. But before ridiculing an organisation that took certain things to extremes, it should be clearly understood that the Americans conceived the war they were fighting as, in General Eisenhower's words, a "Crusade in Europe". Forced as they were to operate among peoples who had been cruelly impoverished by enemy occupation, they had no wish to requisition from those they liberated.

The American fighting man

Finally, a few remarks must be made on the subject of those who constituted an army which, following a brief period of being broken in, would acquit itself so magnificently in the liberating mission it had been entrusted with.

Its successes are ample demonstration of the quality of the American fighting soldier, his courage under fire, endurance, and devotion to duty. Better still, looking down the list of names of an American company where Anglo-Saxon names, Scottish, Irish, German, Scandinavian, Italian, Spanish (some of Indian ancestry), Slavonic, Greek, and even Japanese, are to be found side by side, tribute is due to the system of education in the United States which has shown itself capable of moulding the son of every immigrant into a citizen and a patriot, whatever his social class, his race, or his religion.

General Marshall himself made the following statement as to the methods by which the American soldier received his training:

"Not only were men taught to handle their weapons with proficiency in the replacement training centres, but they were taught to take care of themselves personally. There was intense instruction in personal sanitation, malaria control, processing of contaminated water, cooking, and keeping dry in the open and all the other lore that a good soldier must understand. But most important, our replacements were taught the tricks of survival in battle.

"Problems of street fighting, jungle fighting, and close combat were staged in realistic fashion with live ammunition, and men learned to crawl under supporting machine-gun fire, to use grenades, and advance under live artillery barrages just as they must in battle."

A ready-made officer corps available

For the officer corps, the climate of competition and free enterprise in America, and its corollary in terms of personal initiative and responsibility, and the massive growth of big business throughout the United States provided a source of hundreds of thousands of reserve officers capable not only of commanding a company or a battalion, but also of undertaking general staff duties. This was helped by the fact that the abilities of every man in civil life were judiciously put to use; an ingenious system of temporary promotion enabled each man to find the post where he would be most effective. There is a significant remark by General Bradley in this connection. Speaking of the lack of enthusiasm felt before the war by fellow comrades of the Regular Army who found themselves posted to information services, and of the errors or miscalculations suffered in consequence in the early stages of the war, he writes:

"Had it not been for the uniquely qualified reservists who so capably filled so many of our intelligence jobs throughout the war, the army would have found itself badly pressed for competent intelligence personnel."

But what is true of this branch of the service is also true of any other, and, as regards the quality of the American reserve officer, what is true of the Army is equally true of the Navy and the Air Force.

Help Them
KEEP YOUR WAR SAVINGS PLEDGE
ISSUED BY U.S. TREASURY DEPT.

◁ *Swamp battle practice in the Pacific theatre.*
△ *Another manifestation of the need by most of the combatants to finance their massive war efforts with war loans, bonds, and savings.*

◁ *Assault landing practice for men of the 32nd Division in Australia.*
△ *America fights back.*

CHAPTER 84

The new Panzers

▽ Albert Speer, one of the most gifted and rational of Nazi Germany's war-time leaders, was born in 1905. He had come to Hitler's notice as an architect, and had then built the new Chancellery in Berlin and the great stadium in Nuremberg. Late in 1942 he succeeded Fritz Todt as Reich Minister for War Production when Todt was killed in an air crash. To Speer must go the credit for the phenomenal survival and later massive growth of the German war economy under the handicaps of Allied bombing and lack of raw materials and oil.
▷ Speer test drives an experimental tank hull across a shallow river bed.

The catastrophe of Stalingrad, which reached its climax on February 1, conditioned the evolution of the German Army during the year 1943. To its effects were added those produced by the defeat of the Axis in North Africa, the collapse of Fascist Italy, and the gathering threat of invasion from across the Channel.

To the annihilation of the German 6th Army, comprising five army corps and 20 divisions of the Wehrmacht, Hitler replied by ordering total mobilisation throughout the Third Reich. Hundreds of thousands of men were called up from offices, businesses, and factories, their places being taken by women or foreigners. At the same time, the production of consumer goods for the German population, which had until then hardly been affected, in the general euphoria of victory, was immediately subjected to draconian restrictions; likewise with traffic on the railways. Taking the place of the celebrated Dr. Todt, as Reich Minister for War Produc-

tion and Armaments, Albert Speer applied his abilities to co-ordinating this tremendous industrial effort, and the results were indeed considerable. The production figures below speak for themselves:

	1942	1943
Rifles	1,370,000	2,244,000
Automatic weapons	317,000	435,000
Mortars	10,500	23,400
Field guns (above 7.5-cm)	12,000	27,250
Tanks	9,395	19,885

With the Luftwaffe, figures tell the same story. During 1942, aircraft output had been 15,556 of all types; for 1943 the figure was 25,527. It is worth noting in this connection that if the figure for bomber output from one year to the other was up by under ten per cent, that of fighters was more than doubled, 11,198 as against 5,565. The air force of the Third Reich had finally switched from an offensive to a defensive rôle, as confirmed by the following figures for the production of anti aircraft weapons: 15,472 2-cm, 3.7-cm, 8.8-cm, and even 10.5-cm for 1942; 26,020 for 1943.

During 1942, R.A.F. Bomber Command, virtually on its own, had dropped 43,000 tons of bombs on the Reich and occupied territories. In 1943, with the help of American strategic bombing, this figure would rise to 157,160 tons. But in spite of the near complete destruction of Hamburg in July and successive bombing raids on the Berlin area from the autumn onwards, it has to be admitted that the Allied air offensive against German industrial production did not reach the objectives set.

Guderian, master of tank warfare

On January 23, 1943, Hitler addressed an appeal "to all workers in tank production" urging them to intensify their efforts; on February 17 he summoned Colonel-General Guderian, who had been unemployed since December 26, 1941, by telephone to his H.Q. in Vinnitsa.

Hitler's purpose was to ask him to assume the functions of Inspector-General of Armoured Troops, in accordance with certain conditions which, at his own

△ *A new breed of tank—the Pzkw V Panther, possibly the war's best tank once its teething troubles were ironed out. The Pzkw V designation was later dropped.*
▽ *A.A. gun production was considerably increased in 1943.*

Contrary to other generals directing different arms, the new inspector of the *Panzerwaffe* came outside the authority of the Chief-of-Staff at O.K.H.; he might of course have had to seek his agreement on questions affecting training and organisation within the armoured units, but he was not placed under his command. This situation naturally enough led to a certain amount of friction between Guderian and General Zeitzler. Furthermore, in arranging that he should be directly subordinate to Hitler, Guderian probably imagined that he had given himself a free hand, seeing the many and possibly conflicting political and military burdens that Hitler had taken on. He little realised how mistaken he was.

At all events, the German armoured corps, which both Hitler and Guderian were willing to consider as the decisive weapon of the war, received a powerful initial impulse, because the man who created the *Panzerwaffe* was not only a theorist of imagination and an experienced tactician, but also an outstandingly practical man to boot. The year 1943 saw the mass production of a new and almost final development of the Pzkw IV, the H model. This was fitted with a 7.5-cm (48 calibre) gun and carried steel aprons to protect its tracks. It gave a good account of itself on different battlefields during the second part of the war, despite the fact that weight had risen from the original model's 17.3 tons to the H's 25 tons.

request, Guderian was allowed to draw up.

"I was sent a message summoning me to a conference with Hitler at 15.15 hrs. that afternoon. I was received punctually at that hour; to begin with Schmundt was present, but later Hitler and I withdrew to his study where we were alone together. I had not seen Hitler since the black day of December 20th, 1941. In the intervening fourteen months he had aged greatly. His manner was less assured than it had been and his speech was hesitant; his left hand trembled. On his desk lay my books. He began the conversation with the words: 'Since 1941 our ways have parted: there were numerous misunderstandings at that time which I much regret. I need you.'"

It was impossible for Guderian not to accept the post offered him at that time of crisis, particularly as the terms of his appointment, which he had Hitler sign on February 28 following, gave him almost complete autonomy:

"The Inspector-General of Armoured Troops is responsible to me for the future development of armoured troops along lines that will make that arm of the Service into the decisive weapon."

"The Inspector-General of Armoured Troops is directly subordinated to myself."

Enter the Panther

The production of the Pzkw V or Panther tank was at a less advanced stage. This tank weighed 43 tons and carried a very long (70 calibre) 7.5-cm gun, which gave its anti-tank shot a muzzle velocity of 3,068 feet per second. The Panther also had beautifully sloped armour, and this proved very effective in defence as it caused projectiles hitting it to ricochet rather than explode or penetrate. The British and Americans were correct in estimating this tank to be the most formidable brought into German service.

It had been intended to equip the Panzer divisions with one battalion of Pzkw IV's and one battalion of Pzkw V's, which would have given it between 136 and 172 machines, according to whether it had 16 or 22 tank companies. But these plans were not adhered to.

The Tiger

As for the Pzkw VI or Tiger, mention of which has already been made, its lack of speed (23½ mph) and its meagre range (under 65 miles), precluded its use at divisional level. Battalions of them were formed, then reserve regiments. But, despite its excellent 8.8-cm gun, the Porsche assault-gun version, the Ferdinand or *Elefant,* had the disadvantage of being unsuitable for close combat as it lacked a forward-firing machine gun.

"Once they had broken into the enemy's infantry zone they literally had to go quail shooting with cannons. They did not manage to neutralise, let alone destroy, the enemy rifles and machine-guns, so that the infantry was unable to follow up behind them. By the time they reached the Russian artillery they were on their own."

The mechanisation and motorisation of the armoured divisions' anti-tank guns and artillery also occupied Guderian's attention. In carrying through this programme he had Hitler's approval. On the other hand, he opposed Hitler in regard to the proliferation of "assault gun"

△ Colonel-General Heinz Guderian, recalled to service after 14 months in the wilderness. As the new Inspector-General of Armoured Troops he was able to rationalise some of Germany's armoured equipment, but he constantly fell foul of Hitler's whims.
◁ The last word in German tanks, the Pzkw VI Tiger. Though too heavy and too slow, its thick armour and heavy armament made it a formidable opponent for Allied tanks.

battalions which had been surreptitiously removed from his authority, and for which, it seemed, the Führer nourished a special, quite unjustified affection. These self-propelled assault guns were intended to support motorised infantry. Guderian was afraid that their manufacture, on the scale intended by Hitler, would adversely affect the production of tanks and tank destroyers, and also that they would be entirely unsuitable for armour versus armour combat as their protection had not been designed with this in mind and was thus poorly shaped ballistically.

Guderian reports that Hitler abounded with more or less nonsensical ideas that he stood out against. For example, the new Inspector-General writes:

"For street fighting Hitler ordered the construction of three Ram Tigers, to be constructed on Porsche's chassis. This 'knightly' weapon seems to have been based on the tactical fantasies of armchair strategists. In order that this street-fighting monster might be supplied with the necessary petrol, the construction of fuel-carrying auxiliary vehicles and of reserve containers was ordered. Hitler also ordered the construction of multiple smoke mortars for tanks and declared that the helicopter was the ideal aircraft for artillery observation and co-operation with tanks."

Hitler and Guderian disagree on tank strategy . . .

Moreover, it was not over a purely technical question that the two men were in conflict. There were divergences from the very beginning in two far more important areas, divergences which became more and more accentuated.

First, there was the overall conduct of the war. Guderian's opinion, voiced at a conference on March 10 at Vinnitsa, was to withdraw the main Panzer units from the front and reorganise them in the rear, and to hold the new weapons described above in reserve until enough of them had been moved up to allow the cumulative effect of mass and surprise to be utilised; hurling them into battle in bits and pieces would achieve no more than betray the secret of their superiority and encourage the enemy to take effective counter-measures. This argument could certainly not be faulted, though its corollary in Guderian's mind was to defer the major

offensive until 1944 and be satisfied with strictly limited objectives in 1943.

Hitler held the opposite view. He was determined to avenge Stalingrad by launching an operation in the spring with the aim of destroying the Soviet forces that had ventured into the Kursk salient. The German military leaders were split between the two conceptions. Field-Marshal von Manstein and Colonel-General Model reached conclusions similar to those of Guderian, though in fact for different reasons; General Zeitzler, Chief-of-Staff at O.K.H., and Field-Marshal von Kluge, commanding Army Group "Centre", urged an offensive. With these divergences, the Führer's point of view predominated.

In this controversy it is difficult to vindicate Colonel-General Guderian because he was only interested in the Eastern Front, and showed no considera-

△ Reichsführer *S.S. Heinrich Himmler*, head of one of the private armies that drained the strength of the Wehrmacht.
◁ Reichsmarschall *Hermann Göring* controlled another, but less capable, private army that leeched strength from the regular forces.
▽ *A military parade in Berlin.*

The German Pzkw VI Tiger I Ausführung H heavy tank

Weight: 56 tons.
Crew: 5.
Armament: one 8.8-cm KwK 36 gun with 92 rounds and two 7.92-mm MG 34 machine guns with 5,700 rounds.
Armour: hull nose 100-mm, front plate 100-mm, lower sides 60-mm, upper sides 80-mm, rear 82-mm, and top and bottom 26-mm; turret mantlet 110-mm, front 100-mm, sides 80-mm, back 80-mm, and roof 26-mm.
Engine: one Maybach HL 210 petrol motor, 650-hp.
Speed: 23 mph on roads, 12 mph cross country.
Range: 73 miles on roads, 42 miles cross country.
Length: 27 feet 9 inches.
Width: 12 feet 3 inches.
Height: 9 feet 4¾ inches.

The German Pzkw V Panther Ausführung A heavy tank

Weight: 44¾ tons.
Crew: 5.
Armament: one 7.5-cm KwK 42 gun with 79 rounds and three 7.92-mm MG 34 machine guns with 4,500 rounds.
Armour: hull front 80-mm, sides and rear 40-mm, top 15-mm, and bottom 20+13-mm; turret front 110-mm, sides and rear 45-mm, and roof 15-mm.
Engine: one Maybach HL 230 petrol motor, 690-hp.
Speed: 34 mph on roads, 15 mph cross country.
Range: 110 miles on roads, 55 miles cross country.
Length: 29 feet 1 inch.
Width: 11 feet 3 inches.
Height: 9 feet 9 inches.

tion for what the Americans and British might attempt in the summer of 1943 or, with far more likelihood, according to reckoning at the time, in the spring of 1944. So much so that in notes he made preparatory to the Vinnitsa conference, he even states the desirability of "abandoning the policy of sending any tanks of recent design to secondary theatres of operations, and relying there on tank units captured from the enemy."

△ △ *Young volunteers take the oath of allegiance on joining a Croatian legion of the* Waffen S.S. The Signal *caption reads: "Young men follow in their fathers' footsteps. The independent state of Croatia is allied to the Axis powers. Her youth fights for the future of Europe. The young soldiers of the Croatian divisions, with their country's coat of arms on their steel helmets, swear allegiance to Adolf Hitler. Their fathers themselves fought, in a spirit of brotherhood, beside the Germans and the Austrians." The major point, that Germany was becoming desperately short of manpower, is entirely ignored.*
△ *German 15-cm guns and their tractors at a review. As the war swung against Germany, more and more emphasis was placed on artillery as a defensive weapon.*

What would have been the outcome had the Führer adopted this proposition? Simply that Montgomery would have broken the front at Caen with the ease of a circus girl on horseback diving through a paper hoop. But Guderian's having been wrong does not mean that Hitler was right: if he found himself forced to take offensive action on the Eastern Front in 1943, without any chance of success being guaranteed him, the reason is that the failure of his strategy of war had left him quite without any freedom of choice and action.

. . . and army reorganisation

In a further sphere, too, there was no possible hope of understanding between Hitler and Guderian. In his views of the organisation of the army, however, Guderian had the support of his fellow officers in their entirety, both on the staff and in the field. In his memorandum dated March 10, 1943 he had protested against the kind of megalomania to which Hitler was addicted and which led Manstein to write that, obsessed with sheer size and intoxicated by figures, "Hitler constantly ordered the creation of

new divisions. The increase in number of our divisions was certainly desirable, but this was done at the expense of existing divisions, which received no reinforcements, and hence were completely drained. Whereas the new divisions paid for their lack of experience with a heavier toll of lives. The most striking instances of this were the Luftwaffe infantry divisions, the S.S., which were always being increased, and finally those known as the *Volksgrenadier* divisions."

Nor was Manstein guilty of exaggeration. At this time, there were cases of divisions being kept at the front even after their battalions, whose full establishment was some 900 officers, N.C.O.s, and other ranks, had been reduced to 100 and even less, without the slightest attempt being made to bring them up to strength.

Manstein also levels a further criticism at the Führer concerning his directives on weapons:

"His interest in anything technological led him to exaggerate the effect of armament. For example, he imagined himself to be able with the help of a few battalions of self-propelled artillery or new Tiger tanks to redress situations where only the engagement of several divisions held out any hope of success.

"There is no question that within the sphere of armament and weapons he was dynamic and intelligent. But belief in his own superiority here had fatal consequences. His constant interference prevented the Luftwaffe from realising its potential in time and his influence certainly delayed the development of rockets and atomic weapons."

It was this persistent and fateful wrongheadedness that made Guderian write:

"It is better to have a few strong divisions than many partially equipped ones. The latter type need a large quantity of wheeled vehicles, fuel, and personnel, which is quite disproportionate to their effectiveness; they are a burden, both to command and to supply; and they block the roads." And he concluded that salvation lay in "avoiding the establishment of new formations: the cadres of the old Panzer and motorised divisions consist of trained men with a sound knowledge of their equipment and are an incalculable asset in re-forming their divisions. New formations can never be of equivalent value." He returned to his theme later, and advocated "the abandonment of plans for the formation of new armoured or motorised divisions, both in the Army and

◁ Part of Speer's increased war production effort – an assembly line in a heavy munitions factory.
△ German workers with a rough steel ingot emerging from a rolling mill. Further treatment was necessary to make it suitable for the armaments industry.
▽ German tank production. But because they were easier to manufacture, assault guns were now preferred to the basically better tanks.

in the *Waffen* S.S., and the assimilation of these divisions, and of the 'Hermann Göring' Division to the war establishment."

But nothing was done about it, as is shown by the following figures, taken from the war diary of O.K.W.

On January 1, 1943, the land forces of the Wehrmacht, taken with the *Waffen* S.S., had 286 divisions, including 27 armoured and 14 motorised, at the front. On the following October 4, there were 328, 282 of them distributed over the different operational theatres (197 on the Eastern Front) and 46 undergoing training at different degrees in Germany and the occupied territories.

Without dwelling further on the question of the infantry, let us turn our attention to the armoured and motorised units. Out of 41 divisions in this category that figured in the German order of battle on January 1, 1943, six were destroyed at Stalingrad (14th, 16th, and 24th Panzer Divisions, and 3rd, 29th, and 60th Motorised Divisions) and four (10th, 15th, and 21st Panzer Divisions and the "Hermann Göring" Panzer Division) in Tunisia. On October 4, we find 39 Panzer and *Panzergrenadier* divisions counted as operational. Hence eight had been reconstituted, while seven

others were in the process of being re-formed. The advice and warnings contained in Guderian's memorandum quoted above could not be any further neglected.

But the consequences were suffered, for it was impossible to make up the losses, amounting to some 500 tanks a month, that were being sustained by the armoured divisions fighting on the Eastern Front. Such losses were compounded by the fact that the Panzer divisions had been thrown into the Battle of Kursk the previous July 5 without having been restored to full strength. So it came about that by the end of the year most of them were no more than shadows of themselves; their little blue flags pinned up on the vast operational map recording the day-to-day situation at O.K.W. nevertheless enabled the so-called Führer to "conduct operations", just as if they still possessed some offensive potential, however slight.

In Italy it was the same story. On the evidence of its own commanding officer, Lieutenant-General Lemelsen, on October 1 the 29th *Panzergrenadier* Division, which had been hurriedly formed from the 29th Motorised Division, was short of the following standard weapons: 33 out of 58 8.1-cm mortars, 17 out of 31 medium and heavy anti-tank guns, 26 out of 42 tracked self-propelled guns, and 29 out of 42 pieces

△ *Armoured cars and light scouting vehicles, the Panzer divisions' eyes. Not being intended to fight except where absolutely necessary, German armoured cars were lighter and less well armed than their Allied counterparts, some of which were as powerful as the older German medium tanks.*
▽ *Goebbels addresses a group of recently decorated soldiers, no doubt about the great work they had done to keep the Bolsheviks at bay, allowing the development of the Third Reich.*

of artillery.

And it was just the same with infantry divisions.

Armies within the Army

There is also the fact that Hitler continued to acquiesce in the development of the private armies that his fellow Nazis, *Reichsführer* S.S. Heinrich Himmler and *Reichsmarschall* Göring, had set up.

At the end of December 1942, there were eight *Waffen* S.S. divisions; a year later there were 17, both operational and in the process of formation, ten of them armoured or motorised (*Panzergrenadier*), comprising around half a million men. With such a rate of increase they could no longer count merely on volunteer recruitment as had been the rule initially. So Himmler got a certain quota of the conscript force made over to him, his recruiting sergeants creaming off any young men over 5 feet 9 inches tall.

Applied to this date and later, the Allies' decision to approximate the *Waffen* S.S.

to a criminal association loses any foundation in law, since, in order for there to be such an association, it would have had to be voluntary. This it was not. In any event, when it came to *matériel* and equipment, the S.S. divisions had first claim, and this did not always correspond to their degree of training. Nevertheless, given their army training, and without in any sense exonerating those among them who perpetrated atrocities, it can truthfully be said that the S.S. fought well.

During the winter of 1941/2, Hitler ordered Göring to prune the Luftwaffe of its excessive numbers so as to put some hundreds of thousands of men at the disposal of the Army. But the *Reichsmarschall* chose to understand the order differently; without its being exactly possible to evade it altogether, he prevailed upon Hitler to let him maintain his authority over the divisions that would thus be formed, so far as training and personnel were concerned. Hence the origin of the "Luftwaffe field divisions" (*Luftwaffenfelddivisionen* or L.F.D.), of which the least that can be said is that, as regards the quality of their leadership and their fighting qualities,

they were far inferior to the Army's infantry divisions.

Even so, 20 of them were formed, and these enjoyed the same priorities in equipment as the *Waffen* S.S., at a time when weapons and *matériel* were becoming scarce at the front. In addition to this, Göring sought and received permission to set up a "paratroop armoured" division under his authority, the "Hermann Göring" Panzer Division, which up till the time Guderian put some order into it, had expanded (like its patron) until there were 34,000 men on its roll.

By adding the Göring divisions to the Himmler divisions, we arrive at a total of 39 out of the 328 divisions comprising the land forces, all of them independent of O.K.H. Was it Hitler's intention thus imperceptibly to replace the old reactionary and aristocratic army by a new National-Socialist army? Such a hypothesis cannot be written off right away.

Faced with Hitler's incurable misguidedness in spite of all the advice wasted on him, the generals and senior staff officers became restive. They realised that Hitler's obstinate refusal to

△ *After an investiture of prominent industralists, the recipients of the awards inspect a guard of honour with Guderian (at the salute). With Guderian is Albin Sawatski, a leading industrialist, with Johannes Holtemeyer, head of a steel works, accompanied by General Sepp Dïetrich of the S.S., behind him. In the background, with the black moustache, is General Galland of the Luftwaffe.*

WAFFEN SS

Eintritt mit vollendetem 17. Lebensjahr
Kürzere oder längere Dienstzeitverpflichtung
Auskunft erteilt: Ergänzungsamt der Waffen-SS, Ergänzungsstelle III
(Spree), Berlin-Charlottenburg, Schloßstr. 18

△ *A recruiting poster for the Waffen S.S. More and more, however, the S.S. had to cream off the best of the Army's draft to increase its numbers.*

appreciate the realities of the situation would bring the army to catastrophe and render the country defenceless before a Soviet invasion; they set about ways and means of eliminating his pernicious influence without causing too much damage. Field-Marshals von Manstein and von Kluge held the view that he would have to be forced to abandon supreme command of the army; but while agreeing as to the aim, they differed as to the means of achieving it.

Manstein wished to use persuasion, and indeed on three occasions he endeavoured to lead Hitler to a more rational appreciation of military command, yet without actually asking him to make way for someone else: "I knew perfectly well," he

wrote, "that Hitler would never accept surrender of command officially. As dictator he could not do so without a loss of prestige that was for him unacceptable. My aim was thus to induce him to continue as supreme commander only nominally, to agree to hand over the actual direction of military operations in all theatres to a chief of general staff responsible to him, and to appoint a special commander-in-chief on the Eastern Front. I shall say more about these attempts which unfortunately remained fruitless. They were particularly delicate for me, since Hitler knew perfectly well that several sections of the army would have liked to see me hold the post of chief of the general staff or commander-in-chief in the East myself."

At all events he refused to resort to force, if rational argument was ineffective in face of the blind resolve of the despot, it being his opinion that a *coup d'état* could only result in a collapse at the front and chaos in Germany. Kluge, on the other hand, did not exclude the use of force, and for this purpose made contact with Colonel-General Guderian, through Major-General von Tresckow, one of his staff officers, whom he trusted entirely. Guderian owed his temporary disgrace in December 1941 to Kluge and declined to see the emissary for reasons of prudence, for he had no confidence in Kluge's integrity. In any case he had other ideas about the reorganisation of the German high command and well before Tresckow's approach to him (at the end of July 1943) he had acquainted Goebbels with his suggestions on the subject, on March 6 during a visit to Berlin. It was his opinion that in view of the confusion caused by the different command responsibilities of O.K.W., O.K.H., *Oberkommando der Marine, Oberkommando der Luftwaffe*, the *Waffen* S.S. high command, and the Ministry of Armaments, it was necessary that Hitler should have a better qualified chief-of-staff than the inconsistent Field-Marshal Keitel.

He did not get his way any more than Manstein had, nor any more than the latter did he consider taking the final plunge when faced by Hitler's blindness.

In any case, the intellectual and moral crisis that we have just described did not spread to the front, where the troops continued to fight with skill and tenacity.

But the circumstances were tragic, as German forces were outnumbered and virtually devoid of air cover.

CHAPTER 85
Rommel's last throw

In an earlier chapter we left the newly promoted General Montgomery exploiting his brilliant victory of November 5, 1942. Despite the torrential rains which, by all accounts, characterised the last weeks of that autumn, and despite the logistical difficulties inherent in such a prolonged pursuit of the enemy, on November 13 he was bypassing Tobruk; on November 20 he had retaken Benghazi; and on December 13, having covered more than 700 miles in five weeks, he stood before the defensive position of Marsa Brega - Marada, which had hitherto thwarted all the attacks of his predecessors. During this time he had put Lieutenant-General Brian Horrocks in command of X Corps, in place of Lieutenant-General Herbert Lumsden, whom he considered insufficiently aggressive, with Lieutenant-General Miles Dempsey taking command of XIII Corps.

But even Montgomery was perhaps ignorant of one aspect of his victory which post-war documents have revealed

to us. Not only had he defeated the Axis armoured forces in pitched battle; he had also destroyed any desire for combat on the part of Rommel, for a period which was to last nearly three months. By so doing he had created further discord between the members of the Pact of Steel; for the end of this year was marked by a bitter quarrel, whose leading disputants were Hitler, Göring, Marshals Cavallero and Bastico, and Field-Marshals Kesselring and Rommel; and since it was this last-named who got his way, Italo-German relations suffered a new – and fatal – deterioration.

In brief, Rommel thought that all was irreparably lost in Italian North Africa, and had already decided on the Wadi Akarit, to the north of Gabès, as the halting point of the retreat he had begun on November 5. However, he had no intention of holding this line, or the rest of Tunisia, at all costs. His thinking at that time is summed up in the notes he wrote when he got back to Europe: "Our

▽ *The end of the road for the Panzerwaffe in North Africa. Not even the arrival of some mighty Pzkw VI Tiger tanks, such as the one seen knocked-out here, could stem the tide of Allied victory. Axis reinforcements were too few and too late, and those that survived the sea crossing from Italy soon fell to Allied air superiority in 1943. Note the Zimmerit anti-magnetic mine paste, identifiable by the ridged appearance it gave to the surface over which it was applied, on the driver's plate.*

object in Tunisia would again have to be to gain as much time as possible and get out as many as we could of our battle-tried veterans for use in Europe. We knew by experience that there would be no hope of supplying and equipping an Army Group in Tunisia, which meant that we would have to try to reduce the fighting troops there to fewer but well-equipped formations. If a major, decision-seeking offensive were launched by the Allies, we would have to shorten the front step by step and evacuate increasing numbers of troops by transport aircraft, barges and warships. The first stand would be in the hill country extending from Enfidaville round Tunis, the second in the Cape Bon peninsula. When the Anglo-American forces finally completed their conquest of Tunisia, they were to find nothing, or at the most only a few prisoners, and thus be robbed of the fruits of their victory, just as we had been at Dunkirk."

Rommel had therefore to reach Tunisia as quickly as possible, so as to be able to surprise the Anglo-American army which had just arrived in Algeria, and inflict a severe defeat on it, which would allow him to gain time. This was the plan he put forward to Hitler in the presence of Field-Marshal Keitel and Generals Jodl and Schmundt. But his final remark "If the army were to remain in Africa, it would be destroyed", was the spark which set off the powder keg. "The Führer flew into a fury and directed a stream of completely unfounded attacks upon us."

At the end of this interview, Rommel, who was travelling in the special train which was taking Göring to Rome, had to put up with the *Reichsmarschall's* presumptuous and sarcastic remarks, and expressed himself quite frankly. "I was angry and resentful at the lack of understanding displayed by our highest command and their readiness to blame the troops at the front for their own mistakes. My anger redoubled when I was compelled to witness the antics of the *Reichsmarschall* in his special train. The situation did not seem to trouble him in the slightest. He plumed himself, beaming broadly at the primitive flattery heaped on him by imbeciles from his own court, and talked of nothing but jewellery and pictures. At other times his behaviour could perhaps be amusing – now it was infuriating."

"He gave birth to the absurd idea that I was governed by moods and could only command when things went well; if they went badly I became depressed and caught the 'African sickness'. From this it was argued that since I was a sick man anyway, it was necessary to consider whether to relieve me of my command."

Hitler, feeling it politically necessary to retain a firm bridgehead in North Africa, accordingly gave Rommel orders to hold

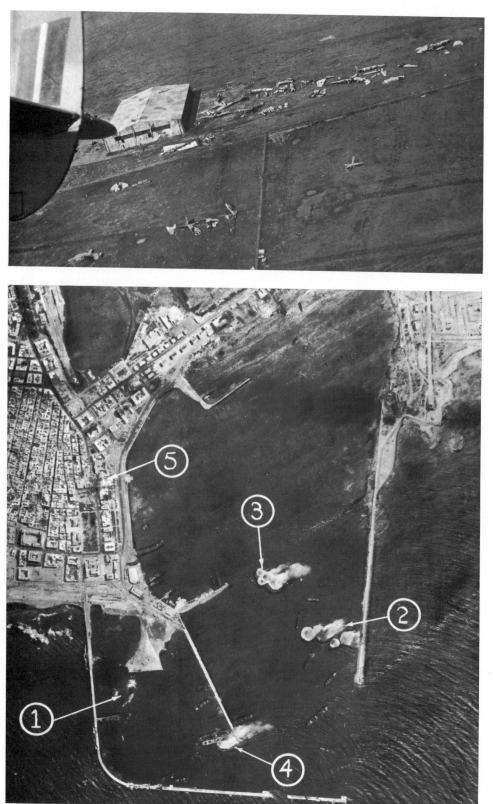

the defensive position of Marsa Brega.

For his part, Field-Marshal Kesselring, although he in no way shared the O.K.W.'s illusions, was equally critical of the almost unseemly haste with which Rommel wanted to leave Libya to its fate. He expected no rapid action from Eisenhower's inexperienced troops, and thought that Montgomery, who was faced with severe logistical problems, would play for safety. It therefore seemed to him quite possible to make the enemy pay dearly, in terms of time, for the advance along the 700-mile road from Marsa Brega to Gabès. As he wrote in his memoirs:

"Of course, it would not be an easy task, but it would have been worthy of a Rommel! And in spite of all the difficulties, it could have been accomplished if Rommel had not been fundamentally opposed to it. His desire to get to Tunisia, and from there, to cross into Italy and the Alps, took precedence over the objectives and orders of his superiors."

Rommel retreats

As may very well be imagined, Marshal Cavallero, in Rome, and Marshal Bastico, in Tripoli, went even further than Kessel-

ring in their criticisms; it is also undoubtedly true that Rommel took no notice of the orders he received from either *Comando Supremo* or the Italian command in Libya, *Superlibia*. It is probably true that it was quite impossible for him to carry out the order he had received to re-establish his position at Sollum-Halfaya, but he also abandoned his defensive position at Marsa Brega on the pretext of making a stand at Buerat, at the other end of the Gulf of Sirte. He reached this position on about January 1, but never had any intention of defending it. And yet he wrote in his diary:

"The British commander had shown himself to be overcautious. He risked nothing in any way doubtful and bold solutions were completely foreign to him . . . I was quite satisfied that Montgomery would never take the risk of following up boldly and overrunning us, as he could have done without any danger to himself."

What does this mean? That Rommel was using false arguments to make his Italian superiors think that he was retreating only on account of enemy pressure? But they were not fooled, hence the tension that grew up between Rommel and Marshal Bastico. So much so that when the former flew to O.K.W. headquarters without informing Bastico, the latter complained in the bitterest

△ △ *A Honey light tank leads the advance past a comprehensively destroyed Pzkw IV medium tank. Note the solid shot protruding from the front plate of what was the turret, under the external mantlet.*
△ *Rommel outside Tobruk in early November. Even if his superiors refused to accept that the game was up in North Africa, Rommel did, and prepared his plans accordingly, with a view to saving as many battle-experienced veterans as possible. But* Comando Supremo *had other ideas and Rommel was ordered to fight it out. Was he, despondent as he was after his defeat at El Alamein, the best man for this hopeless task?*

elapsed before the Allies abandoned the theory that there would be a German counter-offensive, with German troops passing freely through Spain to invade Morocco. This menace, imaginary though it turned out to be, had to be countered by posting the American 5th Army, four divisions strong, on the borders of the two protectorates – which until mid-February reduced the strength of the American troops in the theatre of operations to three divisions.

In Algiers, General Eisenhower allowed himself to be drawn into the quicksands of politics, whilst General Giraud, appointed Civil and Military High Commissioner after the assassination of Admiral Darlan on December 24, 1942, saw his authority disputed. His rallying-cry: "One aim, victory!", and his indifference to political considerations cut very little ice with those for whom victory was not the only aim, and he had to fight on two fronts – against the enemies of his country, and against those who challenged his authority.

No unified command

Finally, Allied operations at the front suffered from a certain lack of co-ordination, for though apparently well integrated, and on excellent terms with each other, the French, American, and British units fighting between the Ouargla oasis and the Mediterranean did not come under a single overall command.

General Delay, commanding the East Saharan Detachment at Fezzan, and Lieutenant-General A. Juin, commanding the French troops in Tunisia, were both under the command of General Henri Giraud, whilst General Eisenhower had overall command of the British and American forces of the British 1st Army, commanded by Lieutenant-General K. A. N. Anderson. But both Eisenhower and Giraud were daily inundated by a host of non-military questions they had to solve; to such an extent that Lieutenant-General L. M. Koeltz, who turned to writing the history of the campaign after having played a leading part in it, could write:

"In Algiers, the two commanders rarely saw each other; they communicated through liaison officers whom General Giraud had attached to Eisenhower. As for Franco-British co-operation at the front itself, it was purely fortuitous, the

△ *Pzkw III tanks and munitions on an Italian quayside prior to running the gauntlet of the Sicilian Narrows.*
▽ *Lieutenant-General L. M. Koeltz, commander of the French XIX Corps.*
▷ △ *A German tank blows up as a British shell finds its ammunition stowage.*
▷ ▽ *Marmon-Herrington armoured cars of a Free French column operating on Montgomery's desert flank.*

terms to Marshal Cavallero:

"His departure constitutes an act of flagrant indiscipline, and wilful disregard of my authority as Supreme Commander and Governor-General. Had any Italian general done that, he would immediately have been court-martialled for deserting his post in front of the enemy."

The reason the Allies had to wait from November 8, 1942 until May 13, 1943 before Axis resistance in North Africa was finally crushed, and the last remnants mopped up at Sainte Marie du Zit, was that all sorts of pressures influenced Eisenhower's operations.

Firstly, the plan which had come out of the deliberations of the British and American Chiefs-of-Staff was a very timid one: no landings were to take place east of Algiers, so that Tunis, the objective of Operation "Torch", was almost 400 miles away from the nearest Allied troops.

Secondly, there was what can only be described as the "Spanish obsession", which haunted both the Foreign Office and the State Department. As a result of faulty Intelligence from British and American agents in Madrid, three months result of instant and very often hasty agreements."

Not wanting the French troops to take their orders from the British 1st Army, General Giraud was content with a "two-headed" arrangement, and General Eisenhower could hardly ask his French opposite number to go back on the terms of the compromise which he himself had proposed at the end of their stormy Gibraltar discussion, and which, according to General Beaufre, laid it down that:

"Upon French territory the French command and the Inter-Allied United Nations command were equal. Each command gave orders to its own troops, but acted by common agreement, and consulted with each other on all important questions. If operations involving a mixed body of troops were carried out, command went to the general whose troops were in the majority."

At the front, however, this sharing of high command created serious difficulties. Although he had previously been severely reprimanded by his superior for having argued the case for a unified command, General Juin, in a long letter on January 1, 1943, brought the matter up with General Giraud once more, putting the case with courage and common sense. It was true, he stated, that for some time he had been able to count on the help of General Anderson. "But that doesn't solve the problem", he added, "for it is once more essential to insist upon there being a single overall commander. There is little point in my having British troops available to me for a single operation, if the essential act is left undone, i.e., if there is no co-ordination of our efforts. I might achieve a local success in drawing the bulk of the enemy's reserves, but the overall objective will not have been achieved. We must therefore have one single command, and if you have not got this matter in hand, as would be desirable, or if for political reasons, or because of previous promises that Eisenhower has hinted at to me, it *has* to be Anderson, then we must agree, as I am willing to do myself, to place the French army under Anderson's command. That would be a lot better than the present highly ambiguous situation, especially as Anderson is an understanding and honest man; with your persuasion from above and mine from below, he could be prevailed upon to act reasonably."

Events were to show how correct this was, but the lesson cost the Allies dear.

Operation "Satin"

The Anglo-American troops entering the front line between Gafsa and the Mediterranean were covered by the French North African Land Forces. Consisting of troops formerly stationed in Tunisia and the Moroccan Infantry Division, the Barré Group was in positions astride the Medjerda river and level with Medjez el Bab, whilst the French XIX Corps (commanded by General Koeltz and consisting of the "Constantine" and "Algiers" Infantry Divisions, and the "Algiers" Light Armoured Brigade) first positioned itself east of Tébessa and then on the Eastern Dorsale, a mountainous fold dominating the coastal plain with its towns of Kairouan, Sousse, and Sfax. To carry out these tasks, General Giraud and his staff were by no means reduced to the forces that the Rethondes agreement of June 25, 1940 had allowed France to keep in North Africa. Thanks to the endeavours of Generals Weygand and Juin, there were

The British Infantry Tank Mark IV Churchill IV

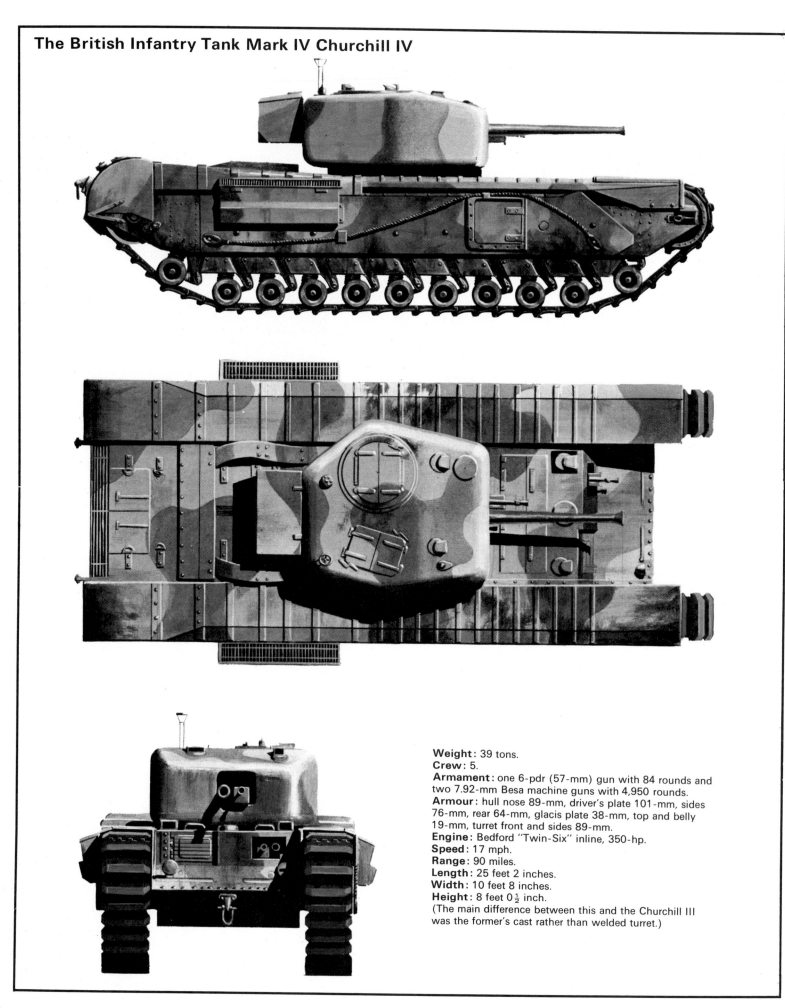

Weight: 39 tons.
Crew: 5.
Armament: one 6-pdr (57-mm) gun with 84 rounds and two 7.92-mm Besa machine guns with 4,950 rounds.
Armour: hull nose 89-mm, driver's plate 101-mm, sides 76-mm, rear 64-mm, glacis plate 38-mm, top and belly 19-mm, turret front and sides 89-mm.
Engine: Bedford "Twin-Six" inline, 350-hp.
Speed: 17 mph.
Range: 90 miles.
Length: 25 feet 2 inches.
Width: 10 feet 8 inches.
Height: 8 feet 0½ inch.
(The main difference between this and the Churchill III was the former's cast rather than welded turret.)

70,000 more troops – officers, N.C.O.s, and men – than the number stipulated; furthermore, out of hiding-places of which the Armistice Commissions were quite unaware, were brought 55,000 rifles, 4,000 automatic weapons, 210 mortars, 43 anti-tank guns, and 82 75-mm guns with ammunition. It should be remembered, however, that since 1939 arms manufacture had made immense strides and that the greater proportion of the arms that the French forces used were out of date, especially the anti-tank guns, and the D1 and Somua tanks with which the light armoured brigades were equipped.

Furthermore, the few motorised vehicles available were at their last gasp, and most could not be repaired for lack of spare parts. On the other hand – and in stark contrast with the *Afrika Korps* – the Americans got delivery of the most modern equipment in record time. When Eisenhower asked for a large consignment of army lorries, he received them in North Africa less than three weeks later. "General Somerwell was still at my headquarters when the message came from the War Department that the last of the trucks had been shipped." The telegram, written by General Somerwell's assistant, Major-General Wilhelm D. Styer, described eloquently the unceasing labour that had gone into the rapid preparing of the convoy, whilst its last few words contained a veiled reproach: "If you should happen to want the Pentagon shipped over there, please try to give us about a week's notice." At all events Eisenhower, taking into account the heavy rains and the state of the terrain, ordered the British 1st Army on December 24 to suspend its offensive towards Tunis for the time being, and a few days later General Giraud was told to dig in on the positions he had already taken up. As soon as possible it was intended to throw in the American II Corps (commanded by Lieutenant - General Lloyd R. Fredendall and comprising the 1st Infantry Division and the 1st Armoured Division) to the right of the French XIX Corps; pushing through to Sfax, it would cut the communications route linking Tunis and Tripoli, thus splitting the Axis forces into two groups which would then be successively annihilated.

This was to be Operation "Satin". It seemed a logical plan, but it would take a long time to execute, and took little or no account of the enemy's capabilities and determination.

The Axis forces

On December 31 the Axis forces in Tunisia stood at just over 47,000 German troops and nearly 18,000 Italians, formed since December 8 into the 5th *Panzerarmee* or Pz. A.O.K. 5, commanded by Colonel-General Hans-Jürgen von Arnim. Under him, on the German side, were the 10th Panzer Division (Lieutenant-General Karl Fischer), which had been stationed in France the previous summer, the 334th Infantry Division (Major - General Friedrich Weber), the Broich Division (Major-General Fritz Freiherr von Broich), which was only of regimental size, and the 501st Tiger Tank Battalion; the Italians provided the XXX Corps (General Vittorio Sogno), comprising the "Superga" Infantry Division (General Dante Lorenzelli), a special brigade, and a few miscellaneous units.

As can be seen, this was an armoured force of very modest dimensions, but to compensate for that, the Luftwaffe had for a few weeks managed to regain mastery of the air above Tunisia. This had two results: firstly, Anglo-American reconnaissance planes were unable to fly over the enemy lines and so did not get wind of Arnim's intentions until it was

△ *A Churchill II on working up exercises in southern Britain. The Churchill I had had a 3-inch howitzer mounted in the hull front and a 2-pdr gun in the turret, but later models were built without the howitzer in the hull, its place being taken by a Besa machine gun. From the Churchill III onwards, the main armament was greatly improved, a 6-pdr being fitted in the III and IV, a 75-mm gun in the IV (North Africa 75), a 95-mm howitzer in the V and VIII, and a 75-mm gun again in the VI and VII. The Churchill's main virtues were good armour and excellent cross-country ability, especially in mountainous terrain, and its major drawback inferior fire-power compared with contemporary German tanks. A total of 5,640 was built.*

Chott el Djerid, where the Germans would have been able to resist the Allies for a very long time.

Arnim attacks

Such is Kesselring's opinion. What is certain is that Arnim could not allow the French forces to remain in possession of the Eastern Dorsale, where an Allied offensive might be unleashed at any moment towards the Gulf of Hammamet. Therefore, on January 18, 1943, the *Gruppe* Weber, comprising the 334th Infantry Division and a few tank units, attacked the positions held by the Moroccan Infantry Division (Brigadier-General Mathenet), which formed the right wing of the Barré Group.

This attack did not really surprise the French, but it did catch them unprepared, for they were very short of reserves (General Giraud, engrossed in his project of forming a powerful North African liberation army, was extremely niggardly in sending reinforcements). Furthermore, against the Weber detachment's brand new tanks, French anti-tank equipment proved quite useless, as is shown by this account of a duel that took place on January 19, between a 55-ton Tiger tank and a 75-mm anti-tank gun:

"Two men worked the gun, Captain Prévot on the elevating-wheel and Sergeant - Major Pessonneau on the sights. When the first tank was 50 yards away, they opened fire. Eight shells either ricocheted off the armour plate, or broke up harmlessly against it. They were about to fire the ninth, when the enemy retaliated with 8·8-cm tracer shells: a shell exploded behind the anti-tank gun, killing the sergeant-major, breaking the captain's left leg, wounding the rest of the gun crew, and overturning the gun."

The Moroccan Infantry Division was badly shaken by this powerful offensive, so Arnim tried to exploit his success by pushing towards the south and south-west and rolling back the XIX Corps' positions facing east. However, an effective, if delayed, counter-attack by Brigadier-General Paul Robinett's Combat Command "B" from the U.S. II Corps prevented the German commander from exploiting at the strategic level an undeniable tactical success which had brought him 4,000 prisoners.

too late; and secondly, German bombers destroyed everything on the routes along which Allied supplies and reinforcements travelled.

This destruction has been painted for us in the memoirs of General Beaufre, who at the beginning of January 1943 left General Giraud's H.Q. to take command of a battalion of crack Moroccan *tirailleurs:* "By day, the roads were the graveyards of vehicles, long lines of which lay riddled with bullets. If you travelled you kept an anxious eye permanently open for enemy planes and dashed for the nearest ditch at the first sign of danger. By night, travelling without lights on badly marked dirt roads, journeys seemed endless and reduced even further the efficiency of our modest forces."

In contrast with Rommel, who was very critical of him, Kesselring, as shown in his memoirs, had nothing but praise for the way in which Colonel-General von Arnim had grasped the purpose of his task and adapted himself to the situation. In his opinion, if Pz. A.O.K. 5 had consisted solely of German troops, Arnim would have been able to push Eisenhower back beyond the Tunis-Algiers border, either as far as the line Bône – Souk Ahras – Tébessa – Tozeur, which would have given the Axis a virtually unassailable position in North Africa, or, failing that, as far as the line Cape Serrat – Béja – Teboursouk –

The Allied command reshuffled

Whilst this fighting was taking place in Tunisia, the Casablanca Conference took place in Morocco, leading to a reorganization of the Allied command structure in the Mediterranean.

Under General Eisenhower's supreme authority, an 18th Army Group was created, consisting of the 1st and 8th Armies, and commanded by General Sir Harold Alexander, whose post as commander in the Middle East was taken over by General Sir Henry Maitland Wilson. The Allied naval forces in the same theatre of operations were to remain under the command of Sir Andrew Cunningham. Air Chief-Marshal Tedder's authority now extended to all Allied air forces in the Mediterranean; in North Africa, particularly, he would have command of Major - General James J. Doolittle's strategic bombers, part of the Western Air Command, and the tactical support formations of Air-Marshal Sir Arthur Coningham's North African Tactical Air Force.

However logical this structure seems, it should be noted that it was never repeated. Both before and after the Normandy landings Eisenhower obstinately resisted the British suggestion that he should have a deputy who would command the Allied land forces, and in this refusal he had the full weight of General Marshall's authority behind him.

At the front, and more or less unknown to General Giraud, the French army detachment was dissolved, and XIX Corps absorbed into the British 1st Army – as had the American II Corps since it had come into the front line. Freed from command, General Juin now took on the job of organising the future French Expeditionary Corps, which he later commanded. Giraud, who had just received from President Roosevelt and General Marshall the promise of enough American aid to equip an army of 11 divisions, acquiesced in this reorganisation of the Allied command: "It was a very big decision to take," wrote General Beaufre later, "since it marked the end of the Gibraltar agreement. The French army now came under Allied command, but had no representation at the highest level, and this situation lasted until 1945." A slightly bitter remark, no doubt, but it must be remembered that the fighting had continually showed the drawbacks of the Gibraltar agreement, and both Generals Koeltz and Juin asked for nothing better than a unified, and hence more effective, command.

△ *A Daimler armoured car softens up an enemy position before the final assault by the waiting British infantry.*

▽ *Fuel for Montgomery's advance: British seamen unload drums of petrol down an improvised ramp. By such means Montgomery was able to keep up the momentum of his advance, much to the surprise of the Axis command.*

△ *A Matilda Scorpion Mark I mine-clearing tank. Twenty-four of these ingenious devices were ready in time for the Battle of El Alamein, and proved invaluable there and on the drive into Tunis. Mounted on the right hand side of a standard Matilda's hull was a compartment housing a Ford truck engine and its operator. This drove, via an extension shaft, a drum mounted in front of the tank on girder arms. The drum revolved, whirling round flails of cable and chain, which set off mines in the tank's path.*

▽ *The Allies' advantage: to Tunis by motor transport.*

Re-enter Rommel

On January 23, 1943, Rommel withdrew from Tripoli; on January 26 he was in Tunisia, inspecting the Mareth Line, whose reinforced concrete defences had been dismantled in accordance with the Franco-Italian Armistice of the Villa Incisa. He had under him the following units:

1. the *Deutsches Afrika Korps* (15th and 21st Panzer Divisions and the 90th and 160th Light Divisions) – or what was left of it;

2. the 16th "Pistoia" Infantry Division and the "Trieste" Motorised Division, which had been brought almost back up to strength during the retreat;

3. the "Giovani Fascisti" Infantry Division, the "Spezia" Airborne Division, and the "Centauro" Armoured Division, all just arrived in North Africa, but in reality far below strength; and

4. the *Gruppe* "Sahara" which had just evacuated the Fezzan, chased out by the indefatigable Leclerc column.

Marshal Cavallero's intention was to place the Axis forces which had just withdrawn from Tripoli (ex - *Deutsch - Italienische Panzerarmee*, ex - *Panzerarmee Afrika*) under Italian command, by placing at their head General Giovanni Messe, who had commanded the Italian XXXV Corps in Russia. Though Cavallero was replaced on January 30 by General Vittorio Ambrosio, his plan was kept, and the very next day General Messe arrived in Tunis as the commander of the new Italian 1st Army or Pz. A.O.K. 1. Rommel wrote of him: "Like most people who came from Russia, he looked on things with considerable optimism. I did not intend to hand over the army until I could feel that its position was reasonably firm for some time ahead."

And in fact it was not until February 20 that General Messe was able to issue his first directive concerning the defence of the Mareth Line. Rommel, however, felt somewhat encouraged to take up this attitude because O.K.W. had not ordered him to return to Germany.

It was in these rather ambiguous circumstances that Rommel launched the last offensive engagement of his African campaigns, and although it resulted in defeat, it nevertheless exemplified his great flexibility as well as his determin-

tion as a military leader. Noting that Montgomery was taking his time in making contact with the German forces at Mareth, he decided to utilise the time thus given to him to deliver a heavy blow on the American II Corps.

He therefore left behind the Italian XX and XXI Corps, as well as his 90th and 164th Light Divisions, relying only on an armoured force consisting of the 10th and 21st Panzer Divisions and the "Centauro" Armoured Division, which he concentrated near Sfax. Here he formed two columns: on the right the two Panzer Divisions, commanded by the *Panzerarmee*'s chief-of-staff, Lieutenant-General Heinz Ziegler, were to launch a surprise attack on the Faïd Pass which cuts through the Eastern Dorsale: and on the left the "Centauro" Division, strengthened by a few *Afrika Korps* units and commanded by Major-General Kurt Freiherr von Liebenstein, who had been borrowed from the 164th Light Division for the duration of the operation, would make a quick dash for Gafsa via Maknassy. The attack began on February 14 and it may fairly be said that for more than a week Rommel's army was in command, although he himself considered that his officers did not give of their best.

The Battle of Kasserine

Stretched out across a very long front, as ordered by the 1st Army, American II Corps had not foreseen where Rommel

would make his attack; and in addition, according to a remark made by Eisenhower himself the day before the attack was launched, there existed at H.Q. an atmosphere of complacency which boded no good. There was a rude awakening. To begin with, Liebenstein forced the 1st Armoured Division (Major-General Orlando Ward) out from the Faïd Pass and inflicted such a heavy defeat that Fredendall had to order his corps to withdraw into the Grande Dorsale. This in turn led to the hasty evacuation of Gafsa, captured by General Ziegler's column in the afternoon of February 15 without a shot being fired. From Faïd and Gafsa, Rommel's two columns converged upon Sbeïtla and attempted to capture the Grande Dorsale.

Although the 21st Panzer Division failed to take the Sbiba Pass, being beaten back on February 20 by the French XIX Corps, the 10th Panzer Division, reinforced by a detachment of the *Afrika Korps*, got through the Kasserine Pass and headed for Tébessa. This further defeat created much tension within the Allied high command; in accordance with the instructions he had received from General Anderson, Fredendall decided to prevent the enemy moving towards Thala, even if that meant surrendering Tébessa which, according to Juin, "was the very nerve centre of his supply system, and plunging north into the mountainous Ouenza region – in heaven knows what disorder. The way to the Constantine region would thus have been opened to Rommel's forces, and he would still have

taken Thala and then le Kef."

In vigorous yet appealing terms, Juin prevailed upon Fredendall to abandon this disastrous idea, whilst at the same time the British 6th Armoured Division (Major-General Charles Keightley) and the artillery units of the American 9th Division, coming from Morocco ahead of their infantry, entered the line to reinforce the Allies' right wing.

Inter-Allied squabbling

In the Axis camp, the twin successes of Faïd and Gafsa sparked off disputes nearly as bitter as those that had taken place among the Allied commanders.

In Arnim's opinion, the Kasserine Pass ought to be considered the final objective of the counter-attack. If it were successful, he would then withdraw the 5th Panzer Division and use it to give himself a little more elbow room in the western and central sectors of the front held by Pz. A.O.K. 5. Rommel, on the other hand, saw bigger and further. He explains his point of view in his notebooks: "I was convinced that a thrust beyond Tébessa by the combined armoured and motorised forces of the two armies would force the

British and Americans to pull back the bulk of their forces to Algeria, thus greatly delaying their offensive preparations. The essential conditions for the stroke to succeed were that it should be made at once and that the striking force should be strong enough to overcome any reviving enemy resistance rapidly and break through to the open road. The thrust northwards had to be made far enough behind the enemy front to ensure that they would not be able to rush their reserves to the passes and hold up our advance. I was satisfied that by holding a number of passes and strategic points

on the roads we would be able to contain the attacks we could expect on our flank. But whether or not the enemy main body would lose the race with my striking force was nevertheless open to question."

Comando Supremo vetoes Rommel's plan

In other words, Rommel, once he had taken Tébessa, would have pressed his attack towards Bône, cutting clean through the British 1st Army's communications; and Kesselring, who had landed in Tunis the previous day, approved his plan, rejecting Arnim's proposals. However, the following evening the Comando Supremo made known its final decision – an attack towards the line Thala–le Kef. "This was an appalling and unbelievable piece of shortsightedness, which did, in fact, ultimately cause the whole plan to go awry," Rommel noted. "A thrust along that line was far too close

to the front and was bound to bring us up against the strong enemy reserves."

And it is a fact that Rommel's attack on Thala failed, the British 6th Armoured Division fighting superbly, and the guns of General Koeltz and the American 9th Division pounding his forces unceasingly. But this failure does not necessarily mean that Rommel would have been successful on a front Tébessa – Bône. Arnim doubted whether he could attain his objective before Montgomery had broken through the Mareth Line. At all events, on February 23, Rommel received a letter appointing him – a little late? – commander of a new Army Group "Africa".

This series of engagements had cost the American II Corps 7,000 men (of whom 4,026 had been taken prisoner), 235 tanks, and 110 self-propelled guns and reconnaissance vehicles; but above all, it was clear that Fredendall had lost the confidence of his men, and on March 6 he handed over his command to Major-General George S. Patton: an excellent choice, for despite his affectation of truculence he was a great leader of men.

◁△ A Crusader tank, fast and manoeuvrable, and therefore always up with the van, harassing Rommel's retreating forces.
◁▽ Motorised infantry streams past an Italian M13/40 knocked out by artillery.
△△ Axis forces halt at the side of a road in the rain. Though the Allies could not be halted by military means, the onset of the winter rains nearly did, and made it unprofitable to continue the pursuit.
△ A patrol of Gordon Highlanders crosses a wadi. With the arrival of the rainy season, such wadis soon filled up and provided all but impassable anti-tank ditches for the retreating Axis forces. Overleaf: British infantry bivouac under the shade of Tunisian trees.

CHAPTER 86
Africa: the end

△ *The commander of a Pzkw IV watches for signs of Allied activity.*

On February 20, 1943 General Alexander, whose new command had got off to such a bad start, called upon Montgomery to lend a hand in easing the enemy pressure on the British 1st Army. Eager to help, Montgomery, whose 51st Division and 7th Armoured Division had just taken the Tunisian townships of Ben Ghardane, Foum-Tatahouine, and Médénine, pushed his advanced forces almost as far as the Mareth Line, which General Messe was holding with six Italian and two German divisions. But on February 22, Rommel, leaving the "Centauro" Armoured Division to cope with the American II Corps, had left Thala and dashed southeast with the 10th and 21st Panzer Divisions.

It can hardly be claimed that Rommel's plan was very original; the Italian 1st Army would engage the British head on, whilst an armoured force consisting of the 10th, 15th, and 21st Panzer Divisions, plus the 164th Light Division, would strike from the Matmata mountains and head for Métameur and Médénine, attacking the enemy from the rear, and driving to the Gulf of Gabès. In other words, a repeat performance of Gazala and Alam el Halfa. But this time the three Panzer divisions, with only 141 tanks,

were two-thirds below strength, and air support, provided by 160 planes (of which 60 were Bf 109 fighters and 20 Stukas), was very meagre. Neither Messe nor Rommel had any great illusions about the eventual success of their attack, which was due to be launched on March 5.

Montgomery halts Rommel

Did the Allies get wind of this Operation "Capri"? Kesselring implies this, and Paul Carell, in his *Foxes of the Desert*, puts forward the same theory. But there is no need to fall back upon such a hypothesis to explain the defeat of the Axis forces in this, their last attempt to secure a change of fortune.

Montgomery knew his Rommel well, and at the first hint of an attack, he regrouped his 2nd New Zealand Division, another infantry brigade, and two armoured brigades, and positioned them on a narrow east-west front between Métameur and Médénine, i.e. at right angles to the line of attack that he thought Rommel would take. Five hundred guns, including many new 17-

pounder anti-tank guns being used in battle for the very first time, lay waiting for the moment to open fire.

As far as the British were concerned, the engagement was no more than an artillery barrage. Firing concentrated and accurate salvoes at the slightest sign of enemy movement within range, the British artillery forced Rommel to break off contact, with the loss of 52 tanks and 640 men killed, wounded, or missing. The British lost one Sherman tank and 130 men. Montgomery expressly forbade his men to pursue the enemy, who retreated behind the Matmata mountains, so the 400 tanks which he had available still remained ready for action.

Paul Carell has described this battle of March 6 grippingly. "The grenadiers, laden with ammunition boxes, had pushed their steel helmets on to the back of their heads. Many of them had cigarettes in the corners of their mouths. They had looked exactly the same in front of the Maginot Line, on the Bug, on the Dniepr, and before Stalingrad.

"When General Cramer visited the tactical headquarters of the 21st Panzer Division, its commander, Major-General Hildebrandt, stood under shell fire with his armoured reserve looking very grave. 'We're making no progress,' he said. But Cramer could see for himself that ahead lay a heavy barrage of fire. British batteries kept up an infernal bombardment against the attacking armour. The stony ground produced a rain of shrapnel with deadly effect on grenadiers and gunners. Major Schlickes' men of the 326th Observer Detachment lay ahead with their sound-rangers and range-finders, trying to pinpoint the artillery positions. The question posed by all the commanders was 'where's all this awful artillery come from?'"

Arnim takes over

Two days later Rommel left Africa for good, but his departure was kept secret, so as not to jeopardise German morale and encourage the enemy. Colonel-General von Arnim succeeded him as C.-in-C. of Army Group "Africa", and tank specialist General Gustav von Vaerst took command of Pz. A.O.K. 5, Major-General Fritz Bayerlein going to General Messe's Italian 1st Army as chief-of-staff.

Meanwhile, O.K.W. had transferred to North Africa the "Hermann Göring" Panzer Division, the "Manteuffel" Division, and the 999th Division, recruited from among military prisoners, who were thus offered the chance of rehabilitating themselves.

But these reinforcements, which raised the number of divisions under Arnim's command to 16, should not deceive us. A number of the divisions were worn out, and the stubbornness of the two dictators forced them to defend a front nearly 400 miles long. Furthermore, it was becoming more and more difficult to supply them from Europe. The Italian merchant navy was, in fact, at its last gasp, as can be seen from the figures which the Communications Minister, Vittorio Cini, laid before Mussolini on March 3, 1943, and which can be summed up as follows:

Situation	Ships	Tons
On June 10, 1940	772	3,292,584
Additions up to March 1943	129	563,068
Total	901	3,855,652
Losses as of March 1943	568	2,134,786
Remaining	333	1,720,866

Deducting further the number of ships

▽ The senior Allied field commander operating against the northern part of the Axis bridgehead, Lieutenant-General K. A. N. Anderson (left), commander of the British 1st Army.

absent from the Mediterranean, liners and ships used for civil and military transport in the Tyrrhenian, Adriatic, and Aegean Seas, and those ships which were in course of repair, less than 300,000 tons were available for the army. And, Cini added, despite the Tripoli evacuation, merchant navy losses through Allied action were continuing at an alarming rate: 87,818 tons in January, 69,438 tons in February.

In March and April the Sicilian Channel lived up to the reputation of the "route of Death" which the Italians had given it. During these two months, out of 132,986 tons of supplies and *matériel* which sailed from Italy, only 77,984 tons got to Bizerta and Tunis, just over a quarter of what Rommel considered necessary to allow the Axis troops to resist a major Allied offensive. This being so, the order given by Hitler and Mussolini to Arnim, after their Klessheim meeting of April 8, 1943, to hold Tunisia at all costs, was pure wishful thinking. However, the view held by Rommel, and later by Arnim, that some of the Axis forces engaged between Mareth and Cape Serrat could be evacuated from Tunisia to Italy, was also rather unrealistic.

On February 21, as the battle for Thala was at its height, General Alexander was briefing his commanders on his strategic

aims. To destroy the enemy forces engaged in Tunisia, he planned that the necessary operations should be subdivided into two phases: firstly the 8th Army would break through at Gabès and join up with the British 1st Army; then together they would crush the enemy by a careful and overwhelming concentration of land, sea, and air power.

The problem was not so much the size of the forces available, which were increasing week by week, but the time limit it imposed on Alexander. If, as the

▽ *Grants forge ahead along a half-submerged road.*
▷ *Sherman tanks (their unit identification markings scratched off the negative by the war-time censor) on the move. With Axis tank strength now at a low ebb, and even the Tigers neutralised by the latest British anti-tank gun, the 17-pdr, Allied armour met little opposition during this last campaign in North Africa. And while the Allies received constant reinforcements, a considerable portion of that which reached the Germans was made up of assault guns, rather than the tanks that were so desperately needed.*

Casablanca Conference had laid down, the Allies were to land in Sicily during the July full moon, the North African campaign would have to be decided by May 15 at the very latest.

On March 14 Alexander completed his briefing with a general directive whose chief quality was its great good sense. It ordered the regrouping of the American, British, and French in separate sectors, the withdrawal of the tanks from their advanced positions, the creating of reserves, and the training of troops. The second part of the directive was devoted to a discussion by Air-Marshal Coningham of air questions, and the co-operation of the air and land forces.

The Mareth Line

On March 20 Montgomery addressed a rousing order of the day to his 8th Army, now up to complete strength. Two of its points are quoted below:

"3. In the battle that is now to start, the Eighth Army:

(a) Will destroy the enemy now facing us in the Mareth position.

(b) Will burst through the Gabès Gap.

(c) Will then drive northwards on Sfax, Sousse, and finally Tunis.

4. We will not stop, or let up, till Tunis has been captured, and the enemy has either given up the struggle or has been pushed into the sea."

At 2230 hours on the same day, the 8th Army's artillery opened fire on General Messe's forces: from right to left, i.e. from the Matmata mountains up to the Gulf

of Gabès, these comprised the XXI and XX Corps commanded by Generals Berardi and Orlando. Thirty minutes later, the British XXX Corps (Lieutenant-General Oliver Leese) attacked the enemy along its coastal sector.

This frontal attack was to be accompanied by a flanking attack carried out by Lieutenant-General Freyberg's New Zealand Corps which, advancing along the corridor bounded on the left by the Grand Erg and on the right by the Matmata mountains, would take the El Hama pass, held by General Mannerini's Sahara group, and dash for Gabès, where he could cut the Italian 1st Army's lines of communication; since El Hamma was 120 miles away from Foum-Tatahouine, Freyberg had begun to advance on March 18. His 2nd New Zealand Division was reinforced by the 8th Armoured Brigade and Leclerc's column. Such was the general aim of Operation "Pugilist".

The results, however, fell far short of the aims proclaimed in Montgomery's order of the day. On the afternoon of the first day, heavy rain had made a quagmire

△ *Allied troops in the ruins of Gafsa in March 1943.*

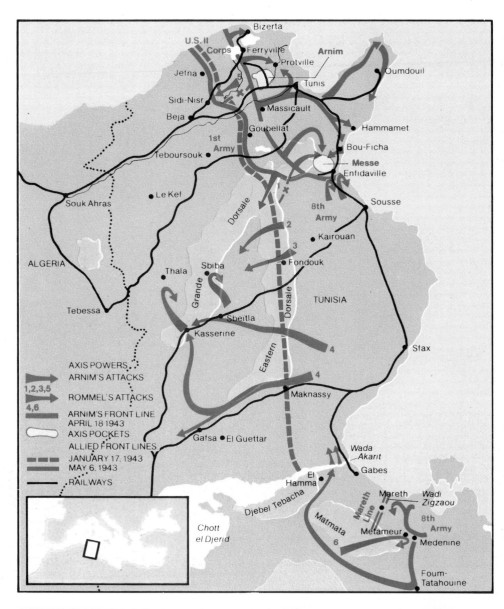

of the Wadi Zigzaou, which flowed in front of the Mareth positions and formed an anti-tank ditch 40 yards wide and 4 yards deep, so that by dawn on March 21, only six of the 50th Royal Tank Regiment's tanks had managed to get through to the opposite side and support Major-General J. S. Nichols's 50th Division, which was having a very bad time under the concentrated fire of the "Giovani Fascisti" Division under General Sozzani. An attempt by the Royal Engineers' bulldozers to breach the bank of the Wadi Zigzaou fared no better. Then the 15th Panzer Division (Major-General Willibald Borowietz), which was being held in reserve, counter-attacked with great vigour: by March 23 the attackers had only one foothold on the left bank.

Faced with this heavy setback, Montgomery declared to Leese: "Never mind, this is where we've got 'em; but you *must* keep the German reserves tied to your corps front."

For he had already decided on another plan. Whilst the 4th Indian Division under Major-General F.I.S. Tuker was attacking the Matmata range on Messe's flank, X Corps and the 1st Armoured Division (Major-General R. Briggs) had been released in the wake of the 2nd New Zealand Division, and in order to deceive the enemy still further, Major-General G. W. E. J. Erskine's 7th Armoured Division had been brought into the front line. Truth to tell, this ruse did not have as much success as had been hoped for it, for by March 21 General Messe had already got wind of Freyberg's move, and had sent the 164th Light Division and the 21st Panzer Division towards El Hamma.

At 1600 hours on March 26, only 20 minutes after the 1st Armoured Division's last tank had entered the line, Lieutenant-General Horrocks gave the signal for the attack, greatly helped by the sun and a violent sandstorm, which blinded the enemy. The trump card, however, was probably the Desert Air Force, which hurled itself at the defence with devastating effect, making use of 22 squadrons of Spitfires, Kitty-bombers, and Hurricane anti-tank fighters, and operating in an area beyond the range of the artillery. "In that area every vehicle", writes Montgomery, "and anything that appeared or moved, was shot to pieces. Brilliant and brave work by the pilots completely stunned the enemy; our attack burst through the resistance and the battle was won."

Messe pulls back

However, the breakthrough at El Hamma took place too late to enable X Corps to reach Gabès before the bulk of the Italian army could be withdrawn. Whilst the loss of 16 infantry battalions, 31 guns, and 60 tanks was a heavy blow, Messe was nevertheless able to regroup his forces in a very strong position along the Wadi Akarit. Here he had only to defend the narrow eight-mile front that lay between the Gulf of Gabès and the lake of Chott el Djerid, and included three hills standing nearly 1,000 feet above the deep furrow that the wadi's high waters had cut into the plain.

Quite rightly, Messe discounted the possibility of a daylight attack on such a strong position; wrongly, however, he supposed that Montgomery would wait for the next full moon, April 19–20, before attacking.

Arnim decides on retreat

Since, as we have seen, time was of the essence, XXX Corps attacked at midnight on April 5, taking advantage of the darkness of the new moon. To avoid any errors they pushed forward in a single line. There was a moment of panic and confusion before the defence steadied itself and inflicted heavy losses on Major-General D. N. Wimberley's 51st (Highland) Division, going over itself to the counter-attack as dawn came up. The following day, at about midday, X Corps' tanks entered the fray, and a few hours later Arnim decided to retreat, a decision he stuck to in spite of Messe's opinion that they were not yet beaten. The battle of Mareth–El Hamma had given the Allies 10,000 prisoners, and Wadi Akarit brought in 7,000 more.

Arnim's decision was probably justified, as a result of the threat that was looming up on the Italian 1st Army's right flank. Here the dynamic General Patton had not taken long to instil a new spirit into both officers and men of his new command. On March 17 he captured Gafsa, and straightway pushed forward toward El Guettar, Maknassy, and Sbeïtla. On April 8, on the Gabès – El Guettar road, he joined up with the 8th Army, whilst on his left, the French XIX Corps moved

towards the Eastern Dorsale. But neither of them was able to intercept the Italian army as it retreated north towards Enfidaville via Sfax and Sousse. This was because of the vast numbers of land-mines that Italian and German sappers had laid, one of which, on April 6, killed the aggressive Major - General Edouard Welvert, commanding the "Constantine" Motorised Division, as they were entering Kairouan.

On April 15, Army Group "Africa" was established along a 135-mile front marked by Cape Serrat, Jefina, Sidi Nsir, Medjez el Bab, Bou Arada, the Djebel Garci mountains, Takrouna, and Enfidaville on the Gulf of Hammamet. To defend this line

△ General the Hon. Sir Harold Alexander, commander of the 18th Army Group and Deputy Allied Commander-in-Chief, North African Theatre.

Arnim had 16 divisions. But what kind of divisions? The Italian Army's historical department, in its work on the Tunisia campaign, gives us the answer.

The "Spezia" Infantry Division and the "Centauro" Armoured Division had been all but destroyed; the "Giovani Fascisti" and the "Pistoia" Infantry Divisions, and the "Trieste" Motorised Division, could muster only 11 battalions and 84 guns between them. The army's total artillery strength consisted of 17 105-mm and 149-mm guns. Nor were the German units under Messe's command any better off: four battalions and a few guns for the 90th Light Division, two battalions and no artillery for the 164th, a dozen or so tanks and three decimated battalions for the 15th Panzer Division. The Pz. A.O.K. 5 was better off but still far from being at full strength. Furthermore, petrol was in such short supply that radio communication was cut down for lack of fuel to drive the generators.

◁△ The final stages of the war in North Africa.
◁▽ Though the final outcome could not be in doubt, the Allies did suffer local reverses, such as the American defeat at the Kasserine Pass, and the constant stream of casualties to be expected in any campaign. The burning wreckage of one such loss, an American Lockheed P-38 Lightning, here forms the background for three German soldiers.
△ British infantry, supported by a Honey tank, continue their advance.

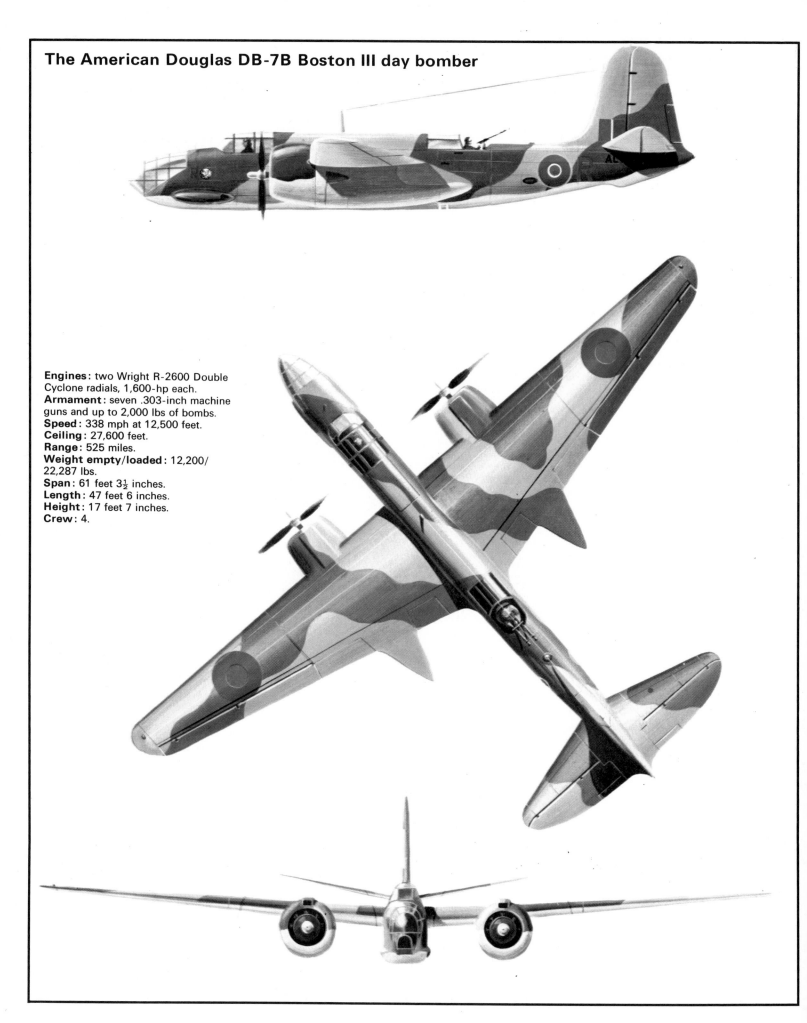

The American Douglas DB-7B Boston III day bomber

Engines: two Wright R-2600 Double Cyclone radials, 1,600-hp each.
Armament: seven .303-inch machine guns and up to 2,000 lbs of bombs.
Speed: 338 mph at 12,500 feet.
Ceiling: 27,600 feet.
Range: 525 miles.
Weight empty/loaded: 12,200/ 22,287 lbs.
Span: 61 feet 3½ inches.
Length: 47 feet 6 inches.
Height: 17 feet 7 inches.
Crew: 4.

The British Supermarine Spitfire L.F. VB fighter-bomber

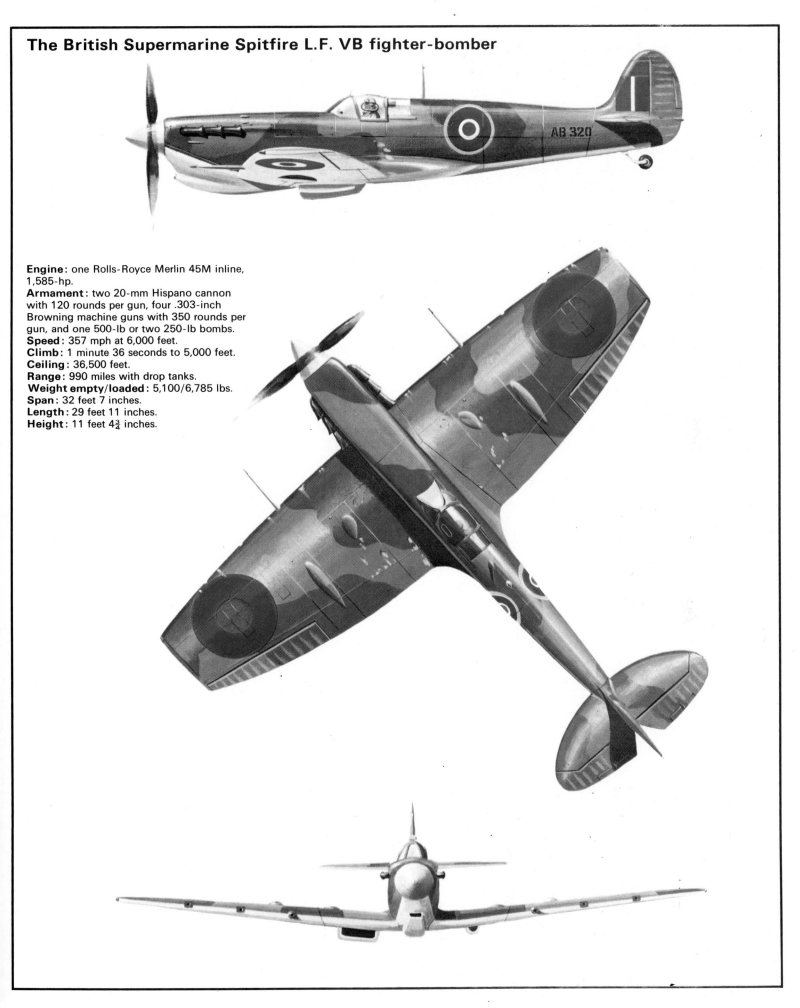

Engine: one Rolls-Royce Merlin 45M inline, 1,585-hp.
Armament: two 20-mm Hispano cannon with 120 rounds per gun, four .303-inch Browning machine guns with 350 rounds per gun, and one 500-lb or two 250-lb bombs.
Speed: 357 mph at 6,000 feet.
Climb: 1 minute 36 seconds to 5,000 feet.
Ceiling: 36,500 feet.
Range: 990 miles with drop tanks.
Weight empty/loaded: 5,100/6,785 lbs.
Span: 32 feet 7 inches.
Length: 29 feet 11 inches.
Height: 11 feet 4¾ inches.

△ American infantry move cautiously into the suburbs of Bizerta, the main port on the north coast of Tunisia.

▽ Alexander's order of the day on April 21. The second paragraph of point 3 was all too true for the Axis – their backs were to the wall, or rather the sea, and only a tiny fraction of their number was to escape to fight again.

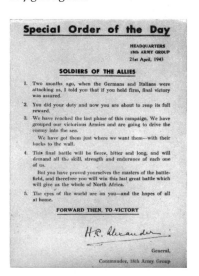

not yet taken it beyond the Gafsa – Fondouk – Maknassy region, whereas ahead of it the French XIX Corps had made contact with the left wing of the 8th Army. As the Americans could not be deprived of their share in the glory of the victory over the Axis, it was decided to transfer them from the right to the left flank of General Anderson's forces – a delicate operation involving as it did the movement of 110,000 men and 30,000 vehicles over a distance of between 150 and 250 miles, through the 1st Army's rear. Begun on April 10, it was concluded without any serious difficulties by April 19, which speaks volumes for the administrative efficiency of General Patton's H.Q.

However, on April 15, Patton took leave of II Corps, being ordered to Rabat, where Eisenhower had entrusted him with the organisation of America's share in Operation "Husky". It was therefore his second-in-command, Major-General Omar Bradley, who was given the glittering prize of Bizerta to aim for; besides his four American divisions, he also commanded a French unit consisting of the African Rifle Brigade and the Moroccan mountain troops of Colonel de Monsabert.

A different story for the Allies

And what of the Allies? During the winter, the British 1st Army had been increased by one corps (IX Corps, under Lieutenant-General J. T. Crocker), and two infantry divisions (the 1st and the 4th). The 8th Army had lost XIII Corps, the 44th Division, the 1st South African Division, and the 9th Australian Division, but had gained the two French divisions, commanded by Major-Generals de Larminat and Leclerc respectively. So including the American II Corps and the French XIX Corps, General Alexander could count on 20 divisions, all equipped (except for the French) with new *matériel* and abundant supplies. This was also the period when the British Churchill Mk. IV tank made its first appearance with the British 6th Armoured Division; it weighed 39 tons, and had a 57-mm gun, whilst its heavy armour allowed it to be used to support the infantry.

The American II Corps' advance had

Dominant rôle for the 1st Army

The lie of the land had led Alexander to entrust the starring rôle in this final operation to the British 1st Army, to which he transferred from the 8th Army the 1st Armoured Division. Its task was to engage the enemy and immobilise its remaining slender reserves by making a strong attack on the southern half of the bridgehead extending from Bizerta to Tunis. The commander of X Corps, Horrocks, was not very happy about the outcome of this diversion because of the very difficult terrain, and his troops were even more pessimistic, in spite of the great reputation as climbers that the Gurkhas of the 4th Indian Division and the Maoris of the 2nd New Zealand Division enjoyed. Events were to prove them right, for April 21 marked a definite setback for the 8th Army which, it is true, captured Enfidaville and Takrouna, but could not break out, being beaten back on the slopes of Djebel Garci, which rise

The German 7.5-cm Sturmgeschütz III Ausführung G assault gun

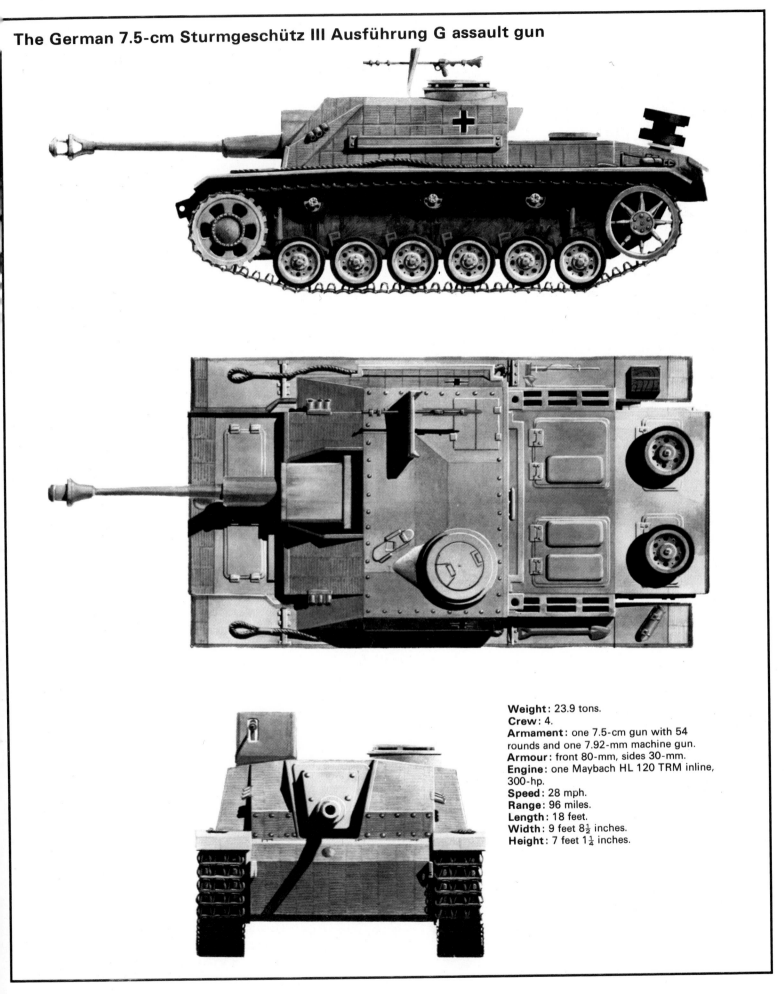

Weight: 23.9 tons.
Crew: 4.
Armament: one 7.5-cm gun with 54 rounds and one 7.92-mm machine gun.
Armour: front 80-mm, sides 30-mm.
Engine: one Maybach HL 120 TRM inline, 300-hp.
Speed: 28 mph.
Range: 96 miles.
Length: 18 feet.
Width: 9 feet 8½ inches.
Height: 7 feet 1¼ inches.

to a height of about 1,600 feet. But the slopes were not the only reason for the defeat. Alexander later wrote of this episode:

"The enemy counter-attacked continuously and, at the cost of very heavy casualties, succeeded in holding the attack. It was noticed that the Italians fought particularly well, outdoing the Germans in line with them . . . In spite of severe losses from our massed artillery fire the enemy kept up his policy of continuous counter-attacks and it became clear that it would cost us heavily to advance further into this tangled mass of mountains. General Montgomery therefore decided late on the 21st to abandon the thrust in the centre and concentrate on forcing the coastal defile."

Final decision in the balance

On the other hand, the French XIX Corps of three divisions, had succeeded in overcoming enemy resistance in the Djebel Fifrine massif (3,000 feet), and on the morning of May 5, approached the western outskirts of Pont du Fahs. At the centre of the British 1st Army, the IX and V Corps had been attacking both banks of the Medjerda river since April 23, and although they had not defeated the enemy, they had at least beaten the Axis forces from the most favourable defensive positions; but each British attack provoked a German counter-attack, such as the "Hermann Göring" Panzer Division's thrust during the night of April 21-22, which cost it 34 out of the 70 tanks it had thrown into the action near Goubellat.

At the head of his II Corps, Major-General Bradley showed himself to be as good a tactician in practice as he had been in theory when an instructor at Fort Benning. By manoeuvring on the heights, he got the better of resistance in the Tine Valley and thus, at just the right moment, was able to release his 1st Armoured Division to cut the Tunis-Bizerta railway line at Mateur, on May 5. And on that same day, on his left, the 9th Division (Major-General Manton Eddy) and the African Rifle Brigade reached the north shore of Lake Achktel, less than ten miles from Bizerta.

On May 6 General Alexander was to deliver the final blow.

Operation "Vulcan"

On April 30, Alexander had detached the 4th Indian Division, the 7th Armoured Division, and the 210th Armoured Brigade from the 8th Army, and allocated them to IX Corps, which had taken up a position between Lake Kourzia and the south bank of the Medjerda; with the wounding of Lieutenant-General Crocker at this time, Lieutenant-General Brian Horrocks, who has given us a colourful description of the episode, took over from him at a moment's notice. To disguise the direction of the attack still more from the enemy, the 1st Armoured Division, operating in the Goubellat area, was reinforced by a large number of dummy tanks. At 0300 hours on the first day of this attack, christened Operation "Vulcan", IX Corps began to advance on a very narrow front, less than two miles wide; the initial attack would be carried out by the 4th Indian Division and the 4th Division, under Major-General J. L. I. Hawkesworth, backed up by the 160 Churchill tanks of the 201st Armoured Brigade; the 6th and 7th Armoured Divisions were to form the second wave. Artillery preparation consisted of the concentrated fire of 100 batteries, whose psychological effect on the enemy was increased by the massive intervention of the whole of the Desert Air Force. Under such a battering, the resistance of the 334th Division and the "Hermann Göring" Panzer Division – or rather what was left of them – soon disintegrated. At 0730 hours, General Horrocks told his armoured divisions to head the advance; that evening there was one last skirmish when 20 tanks of the 15th Panzer Division tried to counter-attack in the Massicault area.

Tunis and Bizerta fall

In the early afternoon of May 7, the 11th Hussars, forming the advance guard of the 7th Armoured Division, entered Tunis. At the same time, the American 9th Division liberated Bizerta, and the 1st Armoured Division bypassed Ferryville and headed for Protville to meet up with the 7th Armoured Division. This link-up, carried out on May 8, led General von Vaerst to send envoys to General Bradley to seek an armistice. The next day

◁ △ The shrinking bridgehead: an Italian armoured car patrol, less than 25 miles from Tunis.
◁ ◁ Elements of the British 1st Army penetrate into the outskirts of Tunis.
◁ ▽ Victorious British infantry arrive on board a Valentine tank.
◁ Major-General von Sponeck, commander of the 90th Light Division (in the front of the car) arrives to surrender to Lieutenant-General Freyberg.
▽ The French high command in North Africa. From left to right: Juin, Catroux, and Giraud.
▽ ▽ Smiles of victory.

the *Panzerarmee* surrendered unconditionally. "The fall of Tunis and Bizerta clearly came to the German Command both in Africa and Berlin, as a most severe shock," Alexander wrote. "It was not until the evening of the 8th May that the High Command issued a statement that Africa would now be abandoned and the 'thirty-one thousand Germans and thirty thousand Italians remaining' would be withdrawn by sea. I commented in a report to General Eisenhower that night that the Navy and Air Forces would interfere with this programme, which in any event depended on the enemy holding a firm bridgehead in Cape Bon, and reminded him of Mr Churchill's words in August 1940: 'We are waiting, so are the fishes.' "

Thus fell the Axis' northern stronghold, which according to Arnim's order should have prolonged Axis resistance in Africa. The southern stronghold, which included the Cape Bon peninsula and the Zaghouan mountains, was cut in two by a raid carried out by the 6th Armoured Division, which found the Hamman-Lif pass undefended and on May 10 reached the

Gulf of Hammamet in the rear of the Italian army. That same day the British V and the French XIX Corps surrounded the Zaghouan mountains and mopped up the remnants of the *Afrika Korps*. Having exhausted its ammunition, the "Superga" Division surrendered to the "Oran" Motorised Division (Major-General Boissau) at Sainte Marie du Zit, and in the Zaghouan mountains the "Morocco" Motorised Division finished off the 21st Panzer Division, and forced the Italian XXI Corps to surrender to General Koeltz. However, XX Corps continued to offer valiant resistance to the British 8th Army. When, on the evening of May 12, the 90th Light Division was crushed at Bou Ficha and forced to surrender, the knell of the Italian 1st Army sounded. In the circumstances, at 1935 hours, Mussolini sent a telegram to General Messe, whose dynamism and skill had greatly inspired his troops: "Cease fire! You are appointed a Marshal of Italy. You and your men have fought the good fight." And his treatment by his victors showed that they were only too aware of his soldierly qualities. Arnim was captured by troops of the 4th Indian Division.

"Masters of the North African shores"

Between May 6 and 13, 130,000 Germans and 118,000 Italians, including 22 generals, surrendered. The French XIX Corps alone took 30,762. Only 638 Axis soldiers succeeded in reaching Italy, among them Lieutenant-General Alfred Gause, Rommel's former chief-of-staff, Bayerlein, Major-General Josef Schmid, commander of the "Hermann Göring" Panzer Division, and General Sogno, commander of the Italian XXX Corps. The Allies, during this seven months' campaign, had suffered 41,133 killed and wounded; 9,310 had lost their lives – 2,156 Frenchmen, 2,715 British, and 4,439 Americans.

On May 13, two days earlier than planned at the Casablanca Conference, General Alexander could send the following restrained but joyful telegram to London:

"Sir, It is my duty to report that the Tunisian Campaign is over. All enemy resistance has ceased. We are masters of the North African shores."

△ *The war in North Africa is finished.*
▽ *The next step – Sicily. This pre-war Italian poster asserts that Bizerta in French hands was a pistol aimed at Sicily. So it was, though the French had no intention of using it. But now it was not just the French. It was the British and Americans, with all their other allies, and they had every intention of firing the pistol.*

BISERTA
IN MANO FRANCESE E
UNA PISTOLA PUNTATA
CONTRO LA SICILIA

CHAPTER 87
Balance of strength

On November 8, 1943, the day following the 25th anniversary of the October Revolution and two days after the liberation of Kiev, a decree of the Praesidium of the Supreme Soviet instituted one more of its large number of distinctions and decorations: the Order of Victory. This order, made of white enamel and encrusted with diamonds, was given only to Front commanders and those who led front-line units.

Apparently, Stalin and his colleagues anticipated the unconditional surrender of the Third Reich by 17 months. Even so, the year 1943 emphasised and added to the defeat suffered by the German armies at Stalingrad and in the great curve of the Don between November 19 and December 31, 1942.

Consideration of the number of days each side was on the offensive during 1943 is clear enough proof of the altered balance of initiative on the Eastern Front: O.K.H. managed 69 days, *Stavka* slightly over two and a half times as many, with 185 days.

Furthermore, it must be remembered that by January 1, 1943 the second Soviet winter offensive had been under way for 43 days, and the third, unleashed on December 24, 1943 would not cease until April 24, 1944, along the line Kovel' – Buchach – Carpathian mountains. In other words, between November 19, 1942 and April 24, 1944, the Russians were on the attack for more than 11 months (334 days).

In addition, O.K.H.'s objectives were becoming more and more modest. It was a long way from Operation *"Blau"* to Operation *"Zitadelle"*, and between the latter and the counter-attack launched on November 16, 1943 by Field-Marshal von Manstein in the Zhitomir sector. In 1944, there would be no German summer offensive.

Growth of Soviet power

The change in the situation was due to the enormous increase in the size of the Red Army during 1943. On June 22, 1941, it had 4,700,000 men under arms. The following December 31, with 2,300,000

◁ *The Soviet Order of Victory. This ornate award was given to Front commanders and leaders of front-line units. It featured a view of Lenin's tomb with the Kremlin and was richly encrusted with diamonds.*
▽ *German artillerymen load a 21-cm howitzer. The weapon was fitted with a dual recoil mechanism, with the top carriage recoiling on the lower portion, while the gun recoiled in its cradle. This made it a very steady mounting.*

△ *Russian cavalry. Tragically vulnerable when used against front line units, it was still an effective arm when used against communications and rear échelon units. After the tanks had broken through, the cavalry was a savage and flexible arm of exploitation which could operate free from fuel and maintenance restrictions.*

men, its numbers had fallen to their lowest level. Two years later they had grown to 5,100,000. Similarly, the number of divisions had increased at the same rate, as is shown in the following table, based on information extracted from Sir Basil Liddell Hart's *The Red Army:*

	June 1941	End of 1942	End of 1943
Infantry divisions	175	442	513
Armoured and mechanised brigades	78	186	290
Cavalry divisions	30	35	41

It must be noted, however, as regards infantry figures, that the figures for 1942 and 1943 include many brigades within the numbers of divisions, so that the effectives available in this arm were far from having tripled, as it might appear at first glance.

Furthermore, the number of guns, in spite of the heavy losses of the 1942 campaign, increased from 5,900 to 19,000, which enabled the Russians to organise 29 artillery divisions, large-scale bodies of artillery unknown in Western armies. These may be said to have been the sledge-hammers used by the front commanders.

As for tanks, in February 1943 there were 7,100 in forward areas, compared with 5,200 at the same time the year before. Moreover, Soviet armour was changing with the entry into service of the T-34/85, in other words a T-34 redesigned so as to be able to mount an 85-mm/53 calibre gun. This fired a 20·4-lb shell at a muzzle velocity of 2,600 feet per second and could pierce German armour at all normal ranges. Of course, the T-34/85 was somewhat heavier than the basic model, but even so, on the road it could still maintain a speed of 32 mph and carry enough petrol for a range of 220 miles. In 1950 this tank showed its superiority, in all aspects, over the improved Sherman tank with which the South Korean army was equipped, and not till 1958 did Soviet factories stop manufacturing it.

Just like Hitler, Stalin attached great importance to the self-propelled gun, so 1943 saw the appearance of the SU-152, a JS chassis armed with a 152-mm gun/howitzer. Its thick armour allowed it to advance in the front line, beside the infantry which it was designed to support with direct fire. However, its weight was 43 tons and its speed was only 15 mph. Of course, its primary task did not require any more of it. Besides the SU-152, there were other calibres of artillery on self-propelled mountings, among which should be noted the SU-85, which was used as an anti-tank gun and can be compared with the "Ferdinand" of the German Army, though much smaller in size.

Though armoured forces had developed so greatly, as the table above shows, the cavalry also made progress and increased in numbers from 30 to 41 divisions between June 1941 and the end of 1943. Forest and marshy regions, where tanks cannot be used, are far more extensive in Russia than anywhere else in Europe. Furthermore, cavalry is ideal for rainy seasons. When earth roads become mud-sloughs, the cavalry can be given major tasks quite impossible for infantry or armoured units. In any case, right until the end of the war, the Soviet Army had no all-purpose cross-country vehicle, comparable with the *Panzergrenadierwagen* or the American half-track. Therefore it was not uncommon for large division- or even corps-size cavalry units to be more useful and speedy at exploiting tank break-throughs than the supposedly more sophisticated motorised infantry.

Many German historians of this campaign are surprised at the ease with which their enemy crossed river obstacles as sizable as the Don, the Donets, and the Dniepr and renewed road communications. They would have been less surprised if they had known that the Red Army had paid considerable attention to its sappers and had created Pioneer and Bridge-builder Brigades. From 17 in the autumn of 1942, their number rose to 46 by the beginning of 1943 and 55 the following summer.

The Soviet land forces possessed an excellent machine for support both in attack and defence: the Ilyushin Il-2m3 "Shturmovik". The armoured bottom of its fuselage could resist 20-mm A.A. shells while it strafed enemy troops with its 23-mm or even 37-mm cannon, bombs, and the rockets with which it was the only aircraft to be armed at the time. The Russians also had the Yakovlev-1 and 9 fighters, the Lavochkin LaGG-3 fighter, and Mikoyan MiG-3 fighter, as well as the excellent Tupolev SB-2 and Petlyakov Pe-2 medium and light bombers. The only Russian four-engined heavy bomber to see widespread service was the Petlyakov Pe-8, but on the whole the Russians stuck to tactical rather than strategic bombing. Only after 1945 did the Soviet Union make a timid entrance into this latter field.

Lend-Lease *matériel . . .*

The question of the support provided by Great Britain and the United States in the gigantic Russian war effort comes in here. At the time, neither of the two enemies at grips on the Eastern Front was very forthcoming in this respect: the Germans so as not to alarm home public opinion by admitting that the U-boat blockade was not as complete as Dr. Goebbels claimed, and the Russians because they have always wished to keep the credit for final victory for the Red Army and the Soviet worker alone.

So, though since then ex-Wehrmacht generals in their memoirs and West German writers in historical works have described the importance of Anglo-American supplies quite openly, the Soviet authors that have been consulted obey an order from on high, thus mentioning the subject only rarely and then somewhat delicately. Occasionally they will make a contemptuous remark concerning the quality of the war *matériel* sent and about the paucity of supply and the

▽ *Three T34/76Bs move easily over a patch of soft ground. Note that the tanks have a very basic finish, no stowage bins, and only one headlight—the Russians concentrated on producing a workmanlike fighting machine without what they regarded as excess fittings.*

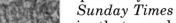

slowness of dispatch.

But the truth, according to statistics quoted by Alexander Werth, at the time *Sunday Times* correspondent in Moscow, is that no less than 9,214 armoured vehicles, 12,230 aircraft, and 4,111 20-mm and 40-mm A.A. guns were supplied to the Soviet Union under the Lend-Lease agreement, all of it, of course, with an adequate supply of ammunition and spare parts. These supplies came from the following countries:

	Tanks	Aircraft	A.A. guns
Great Britain	4,292	5,800	4,111
United States	3,734	6,430	
Canada	1,188		
Totals	9,214	12,230	4,111

It is, nevertheless, true that the Valentines, Matildas, and Grants did no better on the Russian steppes than they had in North Africa against generally superior German tanks. The Sherman tank, as explained above, was not as good as the T-34, even though the armour thicknesses were about the same. The Germans did, however, report large numbers of them in action in the Kurland offensive during the summer and autumn of 1944.

But mechanised warfare is not restricted to armoured and tracked vehicles. By delivering 434,000 trucks, 28,000 jeeps, 5,500 artillery tractors, and 330,000 field telephones, each with three miles of cable, the British and Americans contributed in no small way to increasing the mobility of Soviet land forces.

In the air, the Hawker Hurricanes supplied by the British, the Curtiss P-40 Kittyhawk and Bell P-39 Airacobra fighters and fighter-bombers supplied by the United States, as well as thousands of twin-engined bombers, reinforced the air forces of the Allies' Eastern partner.

These supplies of war *matériel* were accompanied by deliveries of fuel in corresponding amounts: 2,670,000 tons of petroleum products, of which 476,000 tons were high-octane aviation spirit.

Furthermore, with five and a half million pairs of boots and over 25 million yards of cloth for uniforms, the Americans supplied enough to shoe and clothe the entire Red Army once over. With its generous deliveries of flour and tinned food, the U.S.A. were to a large extent responsible for safeguarding its daily rations.

There was more to come, and this would be even more important. It is true that the arms sent under the Lend-Lease agreement totalled only ten or perhaps 15 per cent of those manufactured in Russia, but can it really be believed that Soviet war production could have reached the record figures that Communist historians boast of today, and with good reason, without massive imports of explosives and strategic raw materials, as we call them today? Actually, without relaxing their own armament programmes, the British, Americans, and Canadians supplied the Soviet Union with:

218,000 tons of various explosives
1,200,000 tons of steel
170,000 tons of aluminium
217,000 tons of copper
29,000 tons of tin
6,500 tons of nickel
48,000 tons of lead
42,000 tons of zinc
103,000 tons of rubber
93,000 tons of jute.

Finally, under the industrial heading, can be added 26,000 machine-tools and, from the United States, 1,045 locomotives and 8,260 wagons, built especially for the Soviet Union's broad gauge railways.

Yet these figures do not show all, for certain statistics used do not include shipments after December 31, 1944. Leaving this aside, there is every reason to state that the aid provided was considerable and generously given, particularly so because the safe routes through Persia and Vladivostok were less used than the dangerous and difficult Arctic passage.

The cost of convoys

In all, 42 convoys went to Murmansk and Archangel between August 1941 and May 1945. Their vicissitudes are shown in the following table:

	Convoys	Ships dis-patched	Ships arrived
1941	9	64	62
1942	13	256	185
1943	6	112	105
1944	10	251	242
1945	4	160	158
Totals	42	843	752

Of the 91 which did not reach their destination, 33 had to leave their convoys because of breakdowns and various other reasons. So only 58 ships were destroyed on the way out, but to these must be added those which perished on the way

back, 27 in all, plus six merchant ships travelling alone and five more, victims of Luftwaffe bombing raids on the port of Murmansk. This gives a total of 96.

In warships, convoy escort cost the Royal Navy two cruisers, seven destroyers, and six or seven smaller ships. Such was the price paid by the Western Allies of the Soviet Union to get their convoys to Russia. The least that can be said is that Stalin never understood the enormity of the sacrifice.

Alexander Werth frequently refers to the mutual misunderstandings between the Soviet Union and the Allies over the implementation of the Lend-Lease Act, notably when Admiral Standley complained of the lack of gratitude shown by the Soviet Union towards America:

"It is true that Americans paid for Russian blood with powdered egg and other surplus food. The Russian soldiers liked spam, but they called it, not without some bitterness, 'Second Front'."

In his diary for 1943, Alexander Werth noted on March 9:

"The Russian censorship, after five hours' high-power telephoning, passed the text of the Standley statement. The people at the press department looked furious. Kozhemiako, the chief censor, was white with rage as he put his name to the cable. His mother had died of starvation in Leningrad.... Another Russian remarked tonight: 'We've lost millions of people, and they want us to crawl on our knees because they send us spam. And has the "warmhearted" Congress ever done anything that wasn't in its interests? Don't tell me that Lend-Lease is *charity*!'

◁ ◁ *German fitters strip down the engine of a Pzkw IV during a break in the fighting on the Eastern Front.*
▽ ◁ *Propaganda for the Russians. But after Moscow and Stalingrad the legend of German military might was losing conviction. She had moved to the defensive, and any attacks were now for limited objectives in local areas.*

△ *A Russian 120-mm mortar crew prepares to fire from its neatly dug and camouflaged emplacement. The Soviet Army used a wide range of mortars from 50-mm, through 82- and 120-mm, to a monster 305-mm. These they would mass on a stretch of the front to give a terrifying volume of concentrated fire.*

The Russian Petlyakov Pe-2 bomber, ground attack, and reconnaissance aircraft

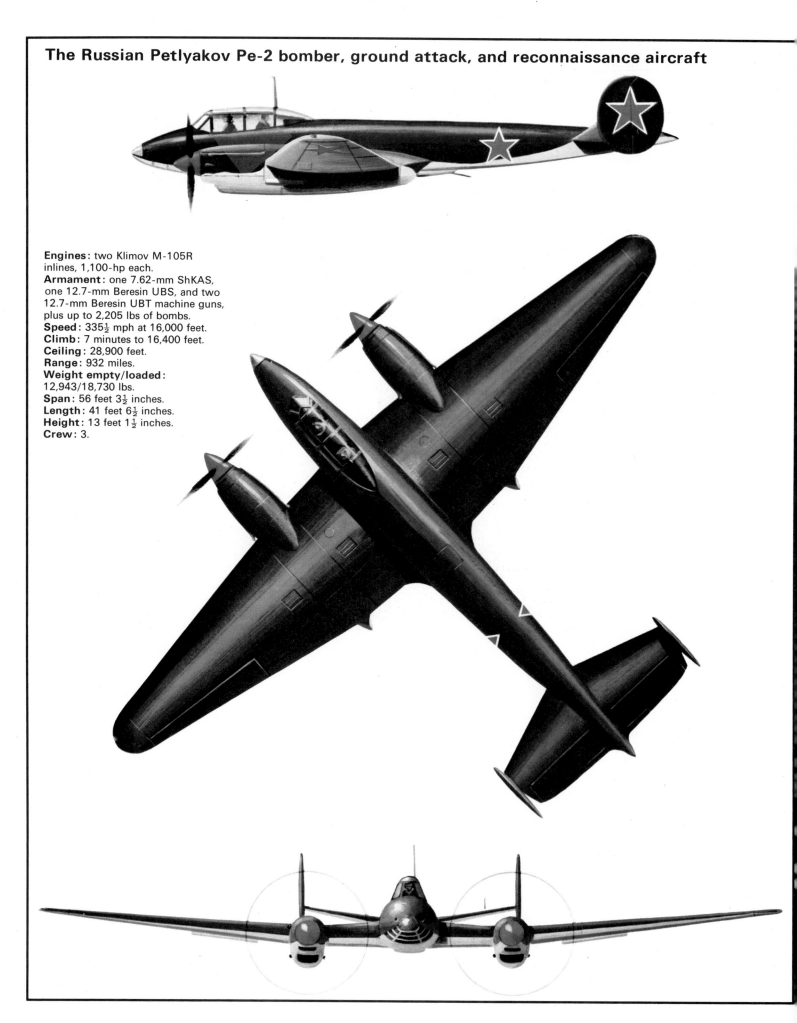

Engines: two Klimov M-105R inlines, 1,100-hp each.
Armament: one 7.62-mm ShKAS, one 12.7-mm Beresin UBS, and two 12.7-mm Beresin UBT machine guns, plus up to 2,205 lbs of bombs.
Speed: $335\frac{1}{2}$ mph at 16,000 feet.
Climb: 7 minutes to 16,400 feet.
Ceiling: 28,900 feet.
Range: 932 miles.
Weight empty/loaded: 12,943/18,730 lbs.
Span: 56 feet $3\frac{1}{2}$ inches.
Length: 41 feet $6\frac{1}{2}$ inches.
Height: 13 feet $1\frac{1}{2}$ inches.
Crew: 3.

The Russian Mikoyan-Gurevich MiG-1 fighter-bomber

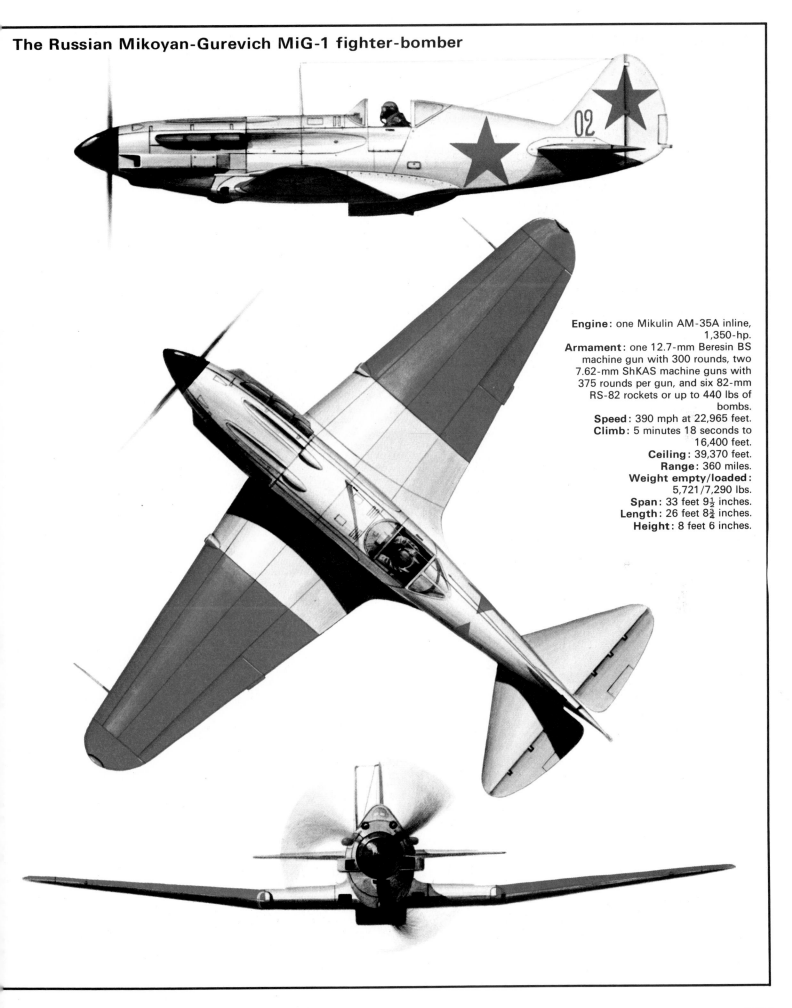

Engine: one Mikulin AM-35A inline, 1,350-hp.
Armament: one 12.7-mm Beresin BS machine gun with 300 rounds, two 7.62-mm ShKAS machine guns with 375 rounds per gun, and six 82-mm RS-82 rockets or up to 440 lbs of bombs.
Speed: 390 mph at 22,965 feet.
Climb: 5 minutes 18 seconds to 16,400 feet.
Ceiling: 39,370 feet.
Range: 360 miles.
Weight empty/loaded: 5,721/7,290 lbs.
Span: 33 feet 9½ inches.
Length: 26 feet 8¾ inches.
Height: 8 feet 6 inches.

"What nettled the British and Americans even more was that, after paying a warm tribute to Soviet Industry, Stalin should have made no mention at all of Lend-Lease and other Western supplies which were now beginning to arrive in very substantial quantities, partly along the newly-reorganised Persian route."

Red Army morale at a high peak

Whatever the quality and quantity of its weapons, the value of an army will always depend to a large measure on the morale, high or low, of the men who serve in its

△ *A patrol of Lavochkin LaGG-3s. By the beginning of 1942 this was numerically the most important type of fighter serving in the East. It carried a variety of weapons including a 23-mm cannon, and when used as escort to the Il-2 assault aircraft was fitted with two 22-gallon long-range tanks. The airframe was adapted late in 1941 to take a more powerful engine which developed into the LaGG-5, a fighter which was flown by many of the leading Russian aces.*

ranks. In terms of this, an examination of the morale factor of the Red Army at the time of the great change in its fortunes of the winter of 1942-1943 is called for.

It would seem that the phrase "Great Patriotic War" goes back to this time. The expression has remained the official name given by Moscow to the German-Soviet hostilities of the years 1941-1945. And so government propaganda appealed to all the traditional values of the Russian nation to hurl it against the "German invader", who was not yet described as "German-Fascist" as he is today. Nobody, not even the Orthodox Church, was exempt from being solicited in this way and, as was its duty in canon law, the

Church did not remain heedless of the call. The proof of it is the column of tanks that it financed through collections, offered to the Russian Army, and baptised after the great prince "Dimitri Donskoi" of Russia who vanquished the Tartars in 1389 on the field of Kulikovo.

Soon the Komintern (or Third International, set up in 1919 to work for world communism) would be dissolved. Though this was certainly a measure aimed at reassuring Roosevelt and Churchill about the purity of Stalin's intentions, and to frustrate Hitler's efforts to involve Europe in a "Crusade against Bolshevism", it was also intended to free the 'Great Patriotic War' from any overtone of "Cosmopolitanism", as the Communists use the term. Doubtless it was for the same reason that the *Internationale* was replaced by a specifically Russian national anthem. In the same patriotic mood, the old battleship *Pariskaya Kommuna* was renamed *Sevastopol*, her original name when launched from the St. Petersburg shipyards in June 1911.

Political commissars abolished

On October 9, 1942 a decree of the Praesidium of the Supreme Soviet dissolved the Corps of Political Commissars, who supervised the actions of commanders down to divisional level and countersigned their orders. In this way a form of surveillance which was always very suspicious, often incompetent, and which seems to have been hated by most of the military hierarchy, was removed. But even so the Commissars were not demobilised; from among them many capable of command were selected to become 200 regimental and 600 battalion commanders, enough men to officer more than 66 infantry divisions by the Western standards of the time.

A shower of decorations

Moreover, the officers had received back their insignia of rank and their long Tsarist-style épaulette boards. A hail of decorations was showered over their uniforms and stimulated their ambition. Six orders were created for the Army and the Air Force and two for the Navy in 1942 and 1943, without counting the Order of Victory mentioned at the beginning of this chapter and the supreme distinction of "Hero of the Soviet Union" dating from 1943. N.C.O.s and privates could be awarded two of these orders as well as a score of medals struck to commemorate the victories of the Red Army.

According to the American historian Raymond L. Garthoff, who may be taken as correct, the total number of decorations awarded by the Soviet authorities in the 'Great Patriotic War' was 11 million while the United States paid their debt of honour to their fighting men with 1,400,049.

On June 22, 1941, the Soviet Army had three Marshals (Voroshilov, Budenny, and Timoshenko); by the end of the hostilities, there were 30 of them, among their number 13 Marshals of the Soviet Union who appear to take precedence over Marshals designated within their branch of the Service: Air Force, eight; Artillery, three; Armoured Forces, four; Engineers, one; and Signals, one. Similarly Admirals Kuznetsov and Isakov were promoted to the rank of Admirals of the Fleet.

Besides these individual distinctions, there were the collective citations which allowed units deserving of it to call themselves "Guards". But this title, which corresponds to the "fourragère" lanyard of the French Army, is not only

◁ A German soldier fills the petrol cans that became known to the Allies as "Jerricans". The Germans produced a range of stamped metal containers for both fuel and ammunition which were superior in design to anything manufactured by their enemies.
▽ Two members of the Luftwaffe Flakartillerie watch a fitter at work on an He 111 on an airfield in south Russia.

△ *A battery of Russian 152-mm gun/howitzers. Captured examples of this gun were used by the Germans in the defence of the Reich at the end of the war. It was also used in the Soviet JSU-152 and KV-2 assault guns.*

symbolic. For the units which merited it it brought considerable advantages in the form of pay supplements and other issues.

The Party and the Army

It can be seen that nationalism was in full flood, the traditional military virtues were restored and set on pedestals and, from a certain point of view, the Army had become the most important thing in the nation. But only to a certain degree, for the Party did not relax its grip on the Army in the slightest. Far from it; the Communist Party had officially recognised cells in all units and bodies of troops, holding meetings even in the cellars of Stalingrad, printing regimental newspapers, recruiting new members, and corresponding with rear organisations. All of these were activities that one would be surprised to see in any Western army but which, it must be stressed, were to the advantage of the military hierarchy. Among the troops Party members were a minority, but they were enjoined to

show an example and were only accepted when they had given evidence under fire of possessing solid military qualities. When necessary, they sought the opportunities to show their ability. So, by September 1, 1944, of 5,400 "Heroes of the Soviet Union" created since the beginning of hostilities, 2,970 were Party members or had applied for membership.

The Communist organisations working within the Army took on another task, that of maintaining permanent liaison between the front and the rear. For example, they used the system of having their battalion or regiment adopted by a certain village, factory, or collective farm. Also, by means of continuous correspondence, they tried to maintain good relationships between the fighting men and what is called the Home Front. Between the military hierarchy and the Communist Party hierarchy, liaison at each level was maintained via Political Officers, who must not be confused with the Commissar for, at least officially, the former had no control over the military commanders. Their task consisted of indoctrinating the troops. Before any important action, the psychological preparation which they carried out was, in all the accounts given, considered as important and mentioned in the same way as the preparations of the staff and of the various technical branches.

"Political work"

One single quotation will be sufficient to illustrate this term. It comes from the monograph written by Colonel V. P. Morosov on the events of the great attack launched on January 13, 1943 by the forces on the Voronezh Front against the Hungarian 2nd Army and the Italian 8th Army:

"The main task of political work," he writes, "consisted of preparing the troops on the basis of the experience of combat obtained in the Stalingrad counter-offensive.

"The political officers of the Front had prepared a plan aimed at ensuring the political security of the attack, by organising the effort of propaganda and agitation.

"First of all, they had to reinforce the strength of the Party and its Youth *(Komsomol)* at all levels. By gaining new Party and *Komsomol* members, new organisations were formed and existing ones were strengthened. The best soldiers and officers joined the Party or the Communist Youth before the battle. The Communists were redistributed among the units in the line. In addition, units and establishments in the rear were required to furnish the front with a certain number of their militants. In this way, the Party's organisations were strengthened within the companies.

"The main mission of the agitation and propaganda was to remind every soldier of the demands of the Party and the Soviet Government: to be ready to inflict a crushing defeat on the enemy. Political agitation was intended to awaken the aggressive spirit in the men and officers and to ensure that tactical orders were successfully obeyed. In the front-line and army newspapers, just as in the sheets produced in the individual companies, the combat mission of the Soviet Army was clearly defined: to free the Soviet homeland from the Fascist conqueror."

At the summit of this double political and military hierarchy stood one man, like the keystone of an arch: Stalin, self-appointed Marshal and Generalissimo of the Soviet Armed Forces on one hand, and on the other Secretary-General of the Communist Party of the U.S.S.R. Did the master of the Kremlin, the greatest opportunist of his time, see further than the needs of the moment when he imposed this form of organisation? The very least that can be said is that once Germany had been defeated no other system would have been better able to guarantee his power, his person, and the régime against the danger of the Soviet military claiming all the credit for the victory and profiting from it.

The extreme rigour of this double discipline should be stressed; in the Red Army, the surrender of a soldier was something absolutely forbidden and in theory inconceivable. This was the cause of the total lack of concern shown for those who had in fact become prisoners. Raymond Garthoff quotes Eisenhower on the subject:

"While talking to a Russian general I mentioned the difficult problem that was imposed upon us at various periods of the war by the need to care for so many German prisoners. I remarked that they were fed the same rations as our own soldiers. In the greatest astonishment he asked: 'Why did you do that?' I said: 'Well, in the first place my country was required to do so by the terms of the Geneva Convention. In the second place the Germans had some thousands of American and British prisoners and I did not want to give Hitler the excuse or justification for treating our prisoners more harshly than he was already doing'. Again the Russian seemed astounded at my attitude and he said: 'But what did you care about men the Germans had captured? They had surrendered and could not fight any more.'"

▽ *A laughing Russian airman holds a bomb painted with the slogan "A present for Hitler!" The picture was probably posed for propaganda purposes, for few front line units would waste time sending friendly messages in this unfriendly form.*

CHAPTER 88
Stalingrad and after

On December 24, 1942, the South-West Front's offensive against Rostov forced the Luftwaffe formations which were supplying the Stalingrad pocket to make a hurried departure from their bases at Morozovsk and Tatsinskaya and establish a new base at Sal'sk, and obliged them to fly over 200, instead of 120, miles to carry out their missions. The retreat of the 4th *Panzerarmee* along the Stalingrad–Novorossiysk railway forced them to withdraw further on January 4, 1943. Now they had to take off from Shakhty and Novocherkassk, some 275 miles from the 6th Army's aerodromes. In this way the development of the strategic situation aggravated the consequences of the criminal irresponsibility with which Göring had boasted of being able to supply the so-called "fortress" at a rate of 500 tons a day. In fact there were only six days between January 4 and 21 during which the unfortunate forces of the besieged army received more than 100 tons of supplies.

The supplying of Stalingrad by air was therefore a failure and one of the most important causes of the surrender. This theme recurs constantly in Field-Marshal Paulus's notes: "You are in fact addressing yourself to men who are already dead", he wrote in answer to a suggestion that he make sorties. "We have stayed here on the orders of the Führer. The Air Force has left us in the lurch and has never kept its promises."

A decision was reached on three drop zones for parachuting supplies behind the divisional sectors, but Paulus objected: "If you insist on parachuting supplies, this army is finished. You must land because our most absolute need is for fuel."

Later, there is a diatribe against Göring: "At the same time I learn from Manstein and Zeitzler that, during a vital meeting, the *Reichsmarschall* said that re-supplying was not going so badly out there! . . . He has big boots so it wouldn't do him any harm to come here himself and see the situation! Clearly my reports have not been passed on to him or he has not taken them seriously. In the old days I should have made my decision at once but now they treat you like a naughty child and what else can you do but grin and bear it?"

Cold and starvation

The situation was serious, as is shown by a note in the O.K.W. war diary, written by its editor at the time, Helmut Greiner. The daily ration of the troops, which Paulus, it must be stressed, also lived on, was by January 10, 1943 as little as: $2\frac{1}{2}$ ounces of bread, 7 ounces of horsemeat (bones included), $\frac{2}{5}$ of an ounce of fats, $\frac{2}{5}$ of an ounce of sugar, and 1 cigarette.

The ordeal of hunger was increased by that of the cold, because, for reasons which have not been elucidated, the winter kit of the 6th Army had not got further than the railway stations of Khar'kov and Kiev. But for weeks, under a bitter north-east wind, the thermometer read between 25 and 35 degrees Centigrade below zero. Artillery ammunition and fuel were in very short supply, which excluded all but very localised counter-attacks.

At the turn of the year, *Stavka* revised its order of battle between the Don and the Volga. Colonel-General Eremenko was required to give up his 57th, 62nd, and 64th Armies to the Don Front which, now consisting of seven armies in all, would take on the task of liquidating the German forces besieged in the Stalingrad pocket. The Russian commander, Lieutenant-General K. K. Rokossovsky, therefore had under his command about 90 brigades and divisions against the 22 decimated and starved divisions of the German 6th Army. Attached to his staff, as representative of *Stavka*, was Colonel-General N. N. Voronov, for whom the destruction of the Germans would mean the baton of a Marshal of Artillery. The 16th Air Army (Major-General S. I. Rudenko) gave the Don Front efficient support and challenged the aircraft of the Luftwaffe which attempted to supply the 6th Army in ever more difficult conditions.

The Russians call for surrender

Preparations for the attack had been completed, when, on January 8, two Soviet officers, carrying a flag of truce, crossed the siege lines, not without some difficulty, and submitted conditions for surrender to Paulus. These had been drawn up and dictated by Voronov and Rokos-

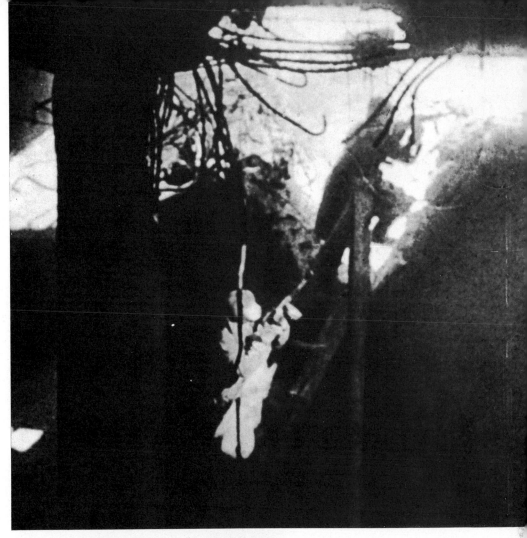

◁ ◁ *Art reflects the reality of war. Exhausted* Gebirgsjäger *slump in a trench and await a Russian attack.*
△ ▽ *Russian defenders in the pulverised remains of Stalingrad's city centre. Fighting floor by floor and even room by room they had trapped and exhausted the 6th Army, and now finally they turned to crush it.*

sovsky in the most formal and proper terms.

"In view," they wrote to him, "of the hopeless situation of the German forces, and to avoid unnecessary loss of life, we suggest the following terms of surrender:

1. All German troops who are besieged, including yourself and your staff, will cease all resistance.

2. All members of the Wehrmacht will surrender by units. All arms, equipment and other property of the Army are to be handed over in good condition.

"We guarantee the lives and safety of all officers, non-commissioned officers and other ranks who cease fire, and, after the war, their free return to Germany or the country of their choice, according to the wishes of the prisoners.

"Wehrmacht troops who surrender will retain their uniforms, rank insignia, decorations, and objects of value. Senior officers will be permitted to retain their swords or daggers. Officers, non-commissioned officers, and other ranks who surrender will receive normal rations at once. Medical care will be given to the wounded, sick, and victims of frostbite."

Previously, Eremenko had tried to use captured German pilots for this purpose. He describes their reaction in these words:

"I brought them together in my headquarters and suggested that they should be sent back to Paulus. 'Make your report and say that you have been shot down and made prisoners, that you have had an interview with the Russian commander of the Stalingrad Front and that Eremenko has promised to guarantee the lives of the whole garrison of Stalingrad, if they surrender.' The pilots asked for a few minutes to consider my proposal. A lively argument arose among them. Some of them

were inclined to accept my suggestion but the majority were opposed to it and soon the former came around to their point of view. Finally, one of the prisoners asked permission to ask a question. I gave it. He said. 'Sir, what would be your reaction if a Russian officer came to you and suggested that your troops should surrender?' 'I should have sent him for court martial,' I replied. 'Well,' he said, 'if we do so, one single mention of surrender and we should be shot out of hand. With your permission we shall not go back to Paulus but shall stay as prisoners, however unpleasant conditions may be.'"

No reply was made to the Russian proposals. But should one accuse Paulus of inhumanity, following the line of historians behind the Iron Curtain, because of his silence and because by that date there was no further point in the 6th Army resisting? This question may be

answered perfectly well by another: what would have happened to the German forces on the Eastern Front as a whole if the defenders of the Stalingrad pocket had laid down their arms on January 9? And the answer given by Field-Marshal von Manstein in his memoirs should be recorded:

"The army had to go on fighting, even if it had no future itself. Every day it gained was of decisive importance for the rest of the German front. It would be quite incorrect to say that the war was finally lost and it would have been better to bring it to a swift end so as to spare suffering. Such a statement would simply be being wise after the event. At that time, it was not at all certain that Germany would lose the war by force of arms. A negotiated peace remained within the realm of possibility, but, in order to achieve this, we had to stabilise the situation on this part of the front,

△ Russian tank riders roar into action on the back of T34/76Bs. Armed with PPSh sub-machine guns, they provided the tanks with instant infantry support. When their tank was knocked out, these troops would simply board another. Their life expectancy was short, but while they lasted they brought the war to the Axis in a terrifying and novel way.

which we did in the end. To achieve this, the 6th Army had to hold down enemy forces locked in battle with it for as long as it could. Cruel necessity forced the High Command to demand this last sacrifice on the part of the valiant troops."

"Die, but save your brother," proclaimed General Dragonmirov, one of the leading lights of the Tsarist Army in the 1880's. Nevertheless, there is no doubt that this pitiless command was imposed on Paulus because of the unbelievable errors committed in the conduct of operations by Hitler and Göring. The *Great Patriotic War* records the reception encountered by the Communist refugees Walter Ulbricht, Erich Weinert, and Willi Bredel in their attempts to suborn the besieged troops with leaflets and radio appeals. It writes: "The men continued to obey Fascist discipline unquestioningly. They did not have the strength to make up their own minds to surrender over the heads of their officers and General."

The only question that arises after reading this is what would the writer of this passage have recorded about the Russian garrison of Brest-Litovsk if it had behaved any differently in July 1941 than did the 6th Army in Stalingrad.

△ *Evacuating Russian wounded. German losses through the cold or wounds were so severe that only 5,000 out of the original 91,000 prisoners survived. About 150,000 Germans and about 50,000 Russians were killed.*
▽ *A Russian assault group in action in a ruined factory.*

The fate of Stalingrad sealed

On January 10, 1943, at 0805 hours, the entire artillery of the Don Front, grouped under the command of Lieutenant-General M. I. Kazakov, with more than 7,000 guns and mortars, opened a torrential fire on the positions of the 6th Army. At 0900 hours, the barrage started to creep forward, thus giving the Soviet 65th and 21st Armies (Lieutenant-General P. I. Batov and Major-General I. M. Chistyakov) the signal to attack. Within three days they had wiped out the Marinovka salient by concentric efforts. By January 17, unleashing his 24th and 57th Armies (Generals I. V. Galinin and F. I. Tolbukhin) on the left and the right, Rokossovsky, who had arrived at Voroponvo, had reconquered two-thirds of the pocket and, most importantly, had taken the aerodrome at Gumrak, the last one still left in German hands, thus preventing German aircraft from landing.

From then on, the remains of the 6th Army were supplied as far as possible by

dropping containers. But the end was close, for the physical and moral resistance of the defenders was becoming rapidly exhausted and, at 1600 hours on January 22, Paulus transmitted the following message to Hitler:

"After having repelled at the outset massive enemy attacks, wide and deep gaps torn in the lines of the XIV Panzer Corps and the IV Corps noon on 22. All ammunition has been exhausted. Russians advancing on both sides of Voroponvo on a 6-kilometre front. Flags waving here and there. No longer any chance of stemming the flood. Neighbouring fronts, also without any ammunition, contracting. Sharing ammunition with other fronts no longer feasible either. Food running out. More than 12,000 wounded in the pocket untended. What orders should I issue to troops who have no more ammunition and are under continuous attack from masses of artillery, tanks, and infantry? Immediate reply essential as signs of collapse already evident in places. Yet confidence still maintained in the command."

Manstein pressed Hitler to answer this telegram, which hinted at surrender, by giving his permission to Paulus to lay down his arms. But three-quarters of an hour of

telephoned appeals did not succeed in weakening the Führer's savage obstinacy. And so, on January 26, as the 21st Army exploited its success of January 22 by pushing eastward, it linked up on Mamaev-Kurgan hill with the Soviet 62nd Army (Lieutenant-General V. I. Chuikov) which had so bravely defended the ruins of Stalingrad. And thus the German pocket was split in two.

In the southern pocket, General von Hartmann, commander of the 71st Division, rashly exposed himself to fire and was killed rifle in hand, while General Stempel of the 113th committed suicide. Their fellow commanders Drebber and Dimitriu surrendered the 297th Division and the Rumanian 20th Division; General von Seydlitz-Kurzbach, commander of the LI Corps, followed their example.

Paulus surrenders

Paulus, on whom, as the end approached, the Führer had conferred the supreme distinction of promotion to Field-Marshal, was by dawn on January 30 trapped in the basement of the large department store in

△ *The triumph of the Red Army.*
▽ *Medals for the defence of Stalingrad (above) and the Caucasus (below).*

△ *The newly appointed Field-Marshal Friedrich Paulus arrives at the Soviet 64th Army headquarters to sign the surrender documents.*
▷ *A Red Army officer observes the military custom of saluting the senior officer of the German party. When Paulus discovered that he could expect civilised treatment from his captors, he relaxed and at lunch proposed a toast for his staff officers, "To those who defeated us, the Russian Army and its leaders."*

▽ *From* Simplicissimus: *the spirit of Stalingrad claims "You think you have beaten me, Stalin. But in the end I will defeat you."*

Stalingrad where he had set up his final headquarters. Together with his staff he accepted the inevitable. General M. S. Shumilov, commanding the Soviet 64th Army, gives the following account of his surrender:

"As our officers entered the room, Paulus was sitting on his bed. According to the accounts given by members of the Russian group, he gave the impression of a man in the last stages of exhaustion. The staff of the 6th Army was given one hour to move out. At that moment Major-General Laskin, Chief-of-Staff of the 64th Army, arrived, with my order to bring Paulus and Schmidt, his chief-of-staff, to 64th Army headquarters at Beketovka.

"A tall, wasted, greying man, in the uniform of a Colonel-General, entered the room. It was Paulus.

"Following the custom under the Hitler régime, he raised his arm as if he were about to give the regulation '*Heil Hitler*' cry. But he stopped himself in time, lowered his arm, and wished us the usual German '*Guten Tag*'.

"General Shumilov requested the prisoner to show his identity documents. Paulus took a wallet out of his pocket and handed the Soviet army commander his military paybook, the usual document carried by German officers. Mikhail Stepanovich looked at it and then asked for other identification confirming that Paulus was in fact the commander of the German 6th Army. Holding these documents, he then asked if it was true that Paulus had been promoted *Generalfeldmarschall*. General Schmidt declared:

"'By order of the Führer, the Colonel-

General was promoted yesterday to the highest rank in the Reich, *Generalfeldmarschall*.'

"'Then can I tell our Supreme Command Headquarters that *Generalfeldmarschall* Paulus has been taken prisoner by troops of my army?' insisted Shumilov, addressing himself to Paulus.

"'*Jawohl*,' came the reply, which needs no translation."

All the same, the northern pocket continued to hold out until February 2, and General Strecker, commanding the XI Corps, was the last to surrender.

Hitler's fury

When he heard the news, Hitler flew into an indescribable rage, the effects of which fill no less than eight pages of the stenographic record that was taken of his statements from 1942 onwards. In Hitler's words, Paulus and his staff had dishonoured themselves by preferring surrender to suicide: "When you have a revolver," he exclaimed to Zeitzler, "it's quite easy. How cowardly you must be to flinch before such a deed! It would be better to allow yourself to be buried alive! It's even worse. Paulus was in a position where he knew that his death would make the other pocket resist even more fiercely. After all, when you give the sort of example he has given, you can't expect men to go on fighting." Zeitzler replied: "There's no excuse. When you feel that you're losing your nerve, then you ought to blow your brains out first." Hitler agreed. "When your nerves give way, there's nothing else for it but [to say] 'I'm at the end of my tether' and kill yourself. One could also say: 'That man must kill himself just as in the old times [leaders] used to rush on their swords when they saw that their cause was irretrievably lost. It's self-evident. Even Varus ordered his slave to kill him.'"

It would not be out of place to reply to this tirade by pointing out that the reincarnation of the foolhardy Varus should be sought not in the cellar of the Stalingrad department store, but in the temporary headquarters at Rastenburg.

In spite of the violent anger which he showed when he heard of the German capitulation at Stalingrad, Hitler for once assumed entire responsibility, as Manstein recalls:

"On February 6 I was summoned to the

Führer's headquarters, although previously I had had no reply to all my requests for Hitler to observe what was going on in our front with his own eyes, or to send for that purpose at least the Chief of the General Staff or General Jodl.

"Hitler began the meeting by saying: 'As for Stalingrad, I alone bear the responsibility. I might perhaps say that Göring gave me an inaccurate picture of the Luftwaffe's capabilities of supplying the Army from the air and so I could possibly make him take some of the blame. But I myself have appointed him to succeed me and so I must accept the responsibility entirely myself.'"

The toll

The cold facts of the matter were that the Russians buried 147,200 German and Rumanian dead in the Stalingrad pocket, while they themselves suffered 46,700 dead, according to Marshal Eremenko. These figures illustrate the savagery of that final battle. The five corps and the 22 divisions (two Rumanian) which perished left in Russian hands slightly more than 91,000 prisoners, including 24 generals and 2,500 officers, as well as more than 6,000 guns and 60,000 motor vehicles. The only troops to escape the trap by being flown out were 24,000 sick and wounded and 18,000 specialists or high-ranking officers marked down for promotion. Of the 91,000 prisoners, very few were still alive in 1950.

After the surrender, the Russians cele-

Field-Marshal Paulus's personal weapon. The Commander of the 64th Army hands it over to the commander of the Stalingrad Front, now happily no longer in existence. I consider that it is yours by right, Andrei Ivanovich.'

"So I took the pistol gratefully, as a symbol of the unforgettable days of the great battle."

The Russians move on

As described above, the defeat of the Rumanian 3rd Army and the Italian 8th Army in the great bend of the Don had forced *Gruppe* "Hoth", which was moving towards the pocket, to suspend its offensive on the evening of December 23, 1942. Already extremely weakened, it was thrown back by Colonel-General Eremenko, who had just been opportunely reinforced by the 2nd Guards Tank Army (Lieutenant-General R. Ya. Malinovsky.) On December 29, Hoth lost Kotel'nikovo, two days later Elista, on the Kalmuk Steppe, and, on January 2, moved back behind the Tsimlyansk–Remontnoye line. Of course, in the battles themselves Hoth had not lost the 571 tanks that the special Moscow communiqué claimed he had, for he had never more than 200 under his command. All the same, the troops of the Russian South Front now saw the road to Rostov open to them. The South Front had replaced the Stalingrad Front on January 2, under the same commander, Eremenko.

△ *With tank support, a group of German soldiers moves off into the winter fog. They are dressed in greatcoats, for despite the pleas of Paulus, the special winter uniforms for the 6th Army remained stacked in railway wagons far behind the lines.*

brated their victory. Recalling the moment, Marshal Eremenko recounts the following story:

"During the evening, at the very modest dinner to which the city council entertained us, General Shumilov, commander of the 64th Army, whose units had taken Field-Marshal Paulus prisoner together with his Staff, handed the German's personal weapon over to Nikita Sergeivich [Khruschev], saying: 'The weapon of the defeated Field-Marshal belongs by right to the commander of the Stalingrad Front, which has taken all the weight of the Nazi attack and also an important part in our counter-offensive.'

"Nikita Sergeivich came to see me on his way back to the front headquarters. I was in bed, with constant and cramping leg pains. Comrade Khruschev gave me an account of his day and then handed me a small burnished metal revolver: 'It's

The Caucasus abandoned

Conditions were worsening day by day. After a long struggle, on the night of December 27–28, Colonel-General Zeitzler had managed to get Hitler to sign an order to Army Group "A", fighting in the Caucasus between Tuapse, Nal'chik, and Mozdok, to begin a full-scale retreat. On January 5 Eremenko was holding Tsimlyansk on the left bank of the Don and was thus 165 miles from Rostov, while Colonel-General von Mackensen's 1st *Panzerarmee* had only just recrossed the Terek, at Prokhladnyy, 365 miles from the same point. In this situation the commander of Army Group "Don", Manstein, would have preferred his fellow-general Kleist to speed up, whereas the latter was retreating slowly and methodically in order to keep his *matériel* and evacuate his depôts properly.

Two circumstances, however, spared Army Group "A" and Colonel-General von Kleist the fate of Paulus and his 6th Army. In the first place, there was no real aggressive pursuit by the Transcaucasus Front's troops, fighting under the command of General I. V. Tyulenev. His Northern Group (Lieutenant-General I. I. Maslennikov), consisting of four armies and two corps of Cossack cavalry, did not succeed in troubling the 1st *Panzerarmee's* retreat to any serious degree, and the Black Sea Group, (Lieutenant-General I. E. Petrov) with its three armies, in spite

of a few local successes, was not able to interfere with the withdrawal of the German 17th Army.

But the most important point was that Manstein's able manoeuvring, on the left bank of the Don and along the Stalingrad–Novorossiysk axis, had put a very successful brake on the advance of Colonel-General Eremenko, which had been very serious for a short time. On January 21, the 2nd Guards Tank Army forced the Manych at Proletarskaya only to be thrown back on the 25th by the 11th Panzer Division, sent in at the right moment by the army group commander under Lieutenant-General H. Balck's excellent leadership. A few days later the German 1st and 4th *Panzerarmee* moved back over the bridges at Rostov together and without too much of a delay. On Hitler's orders, the 17th Army, with eight German and three Rumanian divisions, established itself on the Taman' peninsula, with its right at Novorossiysk, vainly attacked by Petrov in an amphibious operation, and its left backed up against the Sea of Azov.

In fact, Hitler had not given up his Caucasian dream; sooner or later, he thought, the chance would come for him to break out of the bridgehead and seize the Kuban' oil-wells. In vain did Manstein try to put him on his guard against detaching these troops. Since the Hungarian 2nd Army had collapsed completely, broken on the Voronezh Front, the last days of January were ominous with the threat of a second Stalingrad, menacing not only Army Group "A" but also Army Group

△ *American comment: the last kick of the Cossack dance.*

▽ *The remains of the 6th Army shuffles through the ruins of Stalingrad. After the men had been moved to a temporary camp, a typhus epidemic broke out, killing about 50,000 of the exhausted survivors. Many more were to die while being marched to camps in the hinterland of Russia. Here they were put to forced labour and the last of them only returned in 1955. Nearly all the 24 generals who were captured survived their imprisonment, and indeed Paulus became a member of the anti-Nazi "Free Officers' Committee" and made broadcasts over Moscow radio.*

"Don" and Army Group "B"—in other words all those German and satellite forces fighting between Novorossiysk and Kursk.

German disorder

Manstein had his work cut out trying to prevent the armies of the South-West Front (Lieutenant-General N. F. Vatutin) from engulfing *Gruppe* "Hollidt" and crossing the Donets near Kamensk-Shakhtinskiy and Voroshilovgrad, which would have opened the way dangerously towards Taganrog. So the defeat of Army Group "B" burst upon him like a thunderbolt in his headquarters at Stalino.

Overall command of this third act of the Soviet winter offensive had been entrusted to Lieutenant-General F. I. Golikov, commanding the Voronezh Front. His left wing, positioned in the region of Kantemirovka, faced the Italian Alpine Corps and his right, to the north-west of Voronezh, was in contact with the German 2nd Army (Colonel-General von Salmuth). On December 20, 1942 Golikov received orders from *Stavka* to crush the enemy forces between Kantemirovka and Voronezh, principally the Hungarian 2nd Army under Colonel-General Jany.

For this purpose, Golikov divided his forces into three main attack groups. On his left, the 3rd Tank Army (Lieutenant-General P. S. Rybalko) would move out from a line stretching from Kantemirovka

to Novaya Kalitva and push in a north-westerly direction towards Alekseyevka; there it would make contact with the 40th Army of Major-General K. S. Moskalenko, which in its turn would move off from the bridgehead that the Russians had kept at Storogevoye on the right bank of the Don, 100 miles south of Voronezh. In that way the Hungarian 2nd Army would be caught in a pincer while, by using the bridgehead at Bobrov, the XVIII Corps (Major-General Sykov) would attack in the centre and try to cut through the enemy's rear and meet Rybalko's right wing. Although it is true, as the *Great Patriotic War* states, that the attacking forces had superiority only in artillery and armour, their superiority in these two arms must have been considerable.

With two armoured corps and eight armoured brigades, Golikov must have had about 900 tanks to face the 19th and 27th Panzer Divisions and the Hungarian 1st Armoured Division (15 tanks). As for the artillery, it should be noted that when the Russian 40th Army moved out of the Storogevoye bridgehead, its advance was heralded by a barrage laid down by 750 guns and howitzers and 672 mortars, in other words by 179 guns per mile. Furthermore, one-fifth of the Russian artillery, including medium calibre 122-mm and 152-mm guns, fired directly at enemy positions which had been pinpointed for a long time. On January 13, after a ferocious two-hour bombardment, the armour of the Soviet 3rd Tank Army was seen to move forward, 48 vehicles to each mile of front. Success was total. Not only did the Hun-

garian 2nd Army disintegrate under the powerful thrust, but the XXIV Panzer Corps and the Italian Alpine Corps, on the right, were also swept away in the defeat. As a result, by January 19 Rybalko's tanks were already close to Valuyki on the Oskol, 75 miles from their jumping-off point. In addition, the Hungarian rout endangered the German 2nd Army, which was positioned between the Don above Voronezh and the region north of Kursk, linking Army Group "B" with Army Group "Centre" (Field-Marshal von Kluge). To sum up, the break-up of the German front had taken place in a few days over a front of more than 215 miles from Livny to Kantemirovka, while Manstein had no firm positions left on the Donets above Voroshilovgrad.

▽ *A* Sturmgeschütz *III with infantry in their reversible winter uniforms. These suits had a white or a grey or camouflaged face, and were fitted with hoods and draw cords.*

Russian exploitation

At that moment, Colonel-General A. M. Vasilevsky, who had overall command of the Voronezh and South-West Fronts, slipped the leash on his two subordinate commanders. Golikov crashed through the remains of Army Group "B" while Vatutin, on his left, received orders to attack Army Group "Don" across the Donets. Golikov moved swiftly west and south-west and, on February 8, his 60th Army (Major-General I. D. Chernyakhovsky) took Kursk, which had been held against all attacks the previous winter, while his 40th Army moved through Belgorod and Volchansk, and his 3rd Tank Army, further to the south, described

a pincer movement which would give i Khar'kov. Vatutin, passing through Kup yansk, reached the Donets on February 7 crossed it the following day at Izyum and Balakleya, and fanned out south of the river. All in all, the style of campaign o May 12, 1942 was being repeated, but with better chances of success than the previous year for, on one hand, the German armie: had been bled white and on the other, the Russian forces of the South-West Front had Manstein in a trap, both on the Miu: front and on the Donets at Voroshilov grad. In those circumstances, Stalin thought that, on February 6, he could safely order the South-West Front to "Seize Sinel'nikovo with the 6th Army and then, with all speed, Zaporozh'ye, so as to cut the enemy off from all possibility of retreat on the west bank of the Dniep: over the bridges at Dniepropetrovsk and Zaporozh'ye."

In the same tone an order was dispatched to the Voronezh Front to press energetical ly on to Poltava so as to reach the Dniep: near Kremenchug. But, as the *Great Patriotic War* correctly points out, this *ukase* took no account of the losses suf fered by Golikov and Vatutin during six weeks of attacks which had taken them 200 and 240 miles respectively from their supply bases. Some armoured brigades for example, had been reduced to six tanks and some infantry battalions to 20 odd men. Even the better off units were absolutely exhausted.

Hitler confers with Kluge and Manstein

To consider Stalin's order feasible would also imply a complete lack of respect for the preparedness, determination, and boldness of Field-Marshal von Manstein. In circumstances which were close to tragic, Manstein showed himself to be one of the most outstanding tacticians of his time, more than anything because to extract his armies from the serious situation in which they were trapped, he had to fight on two fronts; against the Russians and, moreover, against Hitler. The obstinacy of the latter was no less difficult to combat than the determination of the former.

It had already been seen how the wills of Hitler and Manstein had clashed concerning the mission to be entrusted to the 1st *Panzerarmee* as it retreated from the Caucasus. It was, of course, true that the commander of Army Group "Don" had obtained permission from the Führer to engage it on the Donets after *Gruppe "Hollidt"* had been withdrawn; but it had been obliged to leave behind some of its forces, including the 13th Panzer Division, on the Taman' peninsula. This allowed Vatutin to pursue his outflanking manoeuvre towards Mariupol' on the Sea of Azov.

On February 6, following the defeat of Army Group "B", Hitler summoned Field-Marshals von Kluge and von Manstein to his headquarters at Rastenburg to study the situation. Without making too many difficulties, he authorised Kluge to carry on with Operation *"Buffle"*, which he had been refusing for months. This operation consisted of methodically evacuating the Rzhev salient. With the troops recuperated in this way, he could extend the 2nd *Panzerarmee* southward. It would link up again with the 2nd Army and prevent all enemy attempts to exploit the victories on the Voronezh Front and the Bryansk Front (Lieutenant-General M. A. Reiter) by taking Orel in an outflanking move.

Hitler's discussion with Manstein was more heated. In the latter's opinion, the situation demanded the urgent evacuation of the Don–Donets salient between Rostov and Voroshilovgrad, except that Hollidt would defend the original Mius position and the 4th *Panzerarmee,* once

reformed after being evacuated from the salient, would move swiftly behind the 1st *Panzerarmee* and take up position on its left. In that way there would be a link-up with the *Waffen* S.S. I Panzer Corps, which was arriving at Khar'kov precisely at that moment. The enemy would be prevented from penetrating in the direction of Dniepropetrovsk. However, the decision had to be taken there and then for, given the state of communications, Colonel-General Hoth would need a fortnight to get his forces into place. To all this Hitler replied with involved arguments that the shortening of the front would also benefit the enemy, which was untrue, for the Germans had the advantage of interior lines of communications. Hitler also added that the thaw would once more make the Don and the Dniepr natural obstacles, and so on. In the end, Manstein got his way, but only just.

On February 12, O.K.H. announced that Army Group "B" had been dissolved. This

△ *Panzers in the Caucasus. The troops who had thrust south in July and August 1942 had now to be extracted before they were trapped by the Russian winter offensive. Once more Hitler's reluctance to give up ground made this operation more hazardous than it would have been in normal conditions.*

decision placed the 2nd Army, retreating west of Kursk, under Kluge's orders and gave Manstein authority over the Khar'kov sector, where the *Waffen* S.S. Panzer Corps was in great danger of being encircled by the armies of General Golikov. Should the capital of the Ukraine be evacuated or not? This question gave rise to another tense situation between Army Group "South", which had replaced Army Group "Don", and the Führer's headquarters at Rastenburg. In this case, however, it was settled over the heads of the parties on the initiative of General Hausser, commander of this armoured force, who abandoned the city during the course of February 15 and fell back on the Krasnograd–Karlovka region.

Manstein's view prevails

Two days later, accompanied by Field-Marshal Keitel and Generals Jodl and Zeitzler, Hitler arrived at Zaporozh'ye, to which Manstein had transferred his headquarters. There was a large map of the campaign marked as follows:

1. in the new 6th Army (ex-*Gruppe* "Hollidt") zone, the enemy had crossed the Mius at Matveyev-Kurgan; and
2. in the 1st *Panzerarmee* zone, a cavalry corps had reached the railway junction at Debal'tsevo while at Grishino an enemy armoured column had cut the Voroshilovgrad – Dniepropetrovsk railway line. However, the Soviet drives had been contained in the end and were even being pushed back. By contrast there was a gap of more than 60 miles between Pavlograd and Krasnograd, through which Russian armour was advancing, clearly directed against the elbow of the Dniepr. It was true that with the 4th *Panzerarmee* in line or almost, this corner could be nipped off by pushing the I *Waffen* S.S. Panzer Corps to join Colonel-General Hoth as he moved in.

Hitler was slow to admit this reasoning as, for reasons of prestige, he would have preferred the *Waffen* S.S. to begin its campaign by recapturing Khar'kov. Manstein, however, answered Hitler's points by indicating that the thaw was moving from south to north and a counter-attack in a southerly direction was urgent, leaving aside the question of retaking Khar'kov. Without a southward attack, even if the city was retaken, the Germans

risked being hemmed in by mud. For the third time, Manstein won the battle of words. But even so, in the meantime, General Vatutin's flying columns had reached Novomoskovsk, only 20 miles from Dniepropetrovsk, and also Sinel'-nikovo, 40 miles from Zaporozh'ye. Therefore Manstein sighed with relief when the Führer and his retinue returned to Rastenburg by air on the afternoon of the 19.

Manstein's successes

Army Group "South" unleashed a counter-offensive on February 21. In this it broke the rule which seemed, in the judgement of the most prudent, to sum up the experience of 1918: contain, and only then counter-attack. It is true that there were insufficient numbers of infantry available for containment and that Manstein had command of 13 divisions of armour or of *Panzergrenadiers,* in all about 800 tanks, including a considerable number of Pzkw VI Tigers. But the Russians misunderstood the reshuffling of Manstein's forces. This is how the *Great Patriotic War* describes the situation:

"Both the South-West Front command and Soviet Supreme Command were led to believe from the enemy's retreat from the lower Donets to the Mius and the transfer of his armoured and motorised divisions from around Rostov to near Konstantinovka, that the Germans intended to evacuate the Donets basin and retire behind the Dniepr. That is why Supreme Headquarters kept to its decision to develop its attack as soon as possible".

The result of this error of judgement and of the German initiative was a series of battles and clashes in which the clumsier Russians did not come off best.

On February 22, attacking due south from Krasnograd, the S.S. I Panzer Corps (1st *"Leibstandarte" Panzergrenadier* Division and 2nd *"Das Reich" Panzergrenadier* Division) crushed the Russian forces attacking Novomoskovsk as they advanced; then, reinforced by the 3rd *"Totenkopf" Panzergrenadier* Division of the *Waffen* S.S., the corps pushed on hard towards Pavlograd where it came under the 4th *Panzerarmee,* which Manstein was pushing towards Lozovaya at the same speed. During these strategic moves, Lieutenant-General M. M. Popov's armoured force was utterly destroyed and, with its defeat, the entire South-

The conquerors who stayed behind.
△ *A German soldier, frozen where he fell among the litter of war, bears witness by his inadequate clothing to Germany's unpreparedness for the severity of the Russian winter.*
◁ *One of the orderly cemeteries which the Germans left from Moscow to the borders of the Reich. After Stalingrad the soldier who was sent East was a hero or martyr whose chances of survival were low compared to his comrade in the West.*

West Front behind the Donets was forced into flight.

Khar'kov retaken

Though this retreat was justified in the circumstances (General Vatutin had lost 32,000 killed and captured, 615 tanks, and 423 guns), it nevertheless exposed the left wing of the Voronezh Front, which was now threatened halfway between Khar'kov and Poltava. On March 5, the 4th *Panzerarmee* hit the Soviet 3rd Tank Army hard near Krasnograd. Then a pincer attack enabled the S.S. I Panzer Corps to "lay Khar'kov at the feet of the Führer" on May 14, 1943. *Gruppe* "Kempf", fighting to the north of the city, drove forward at the same time and, on March 18, its *Panzergrenadier* division, the "*Grossdeutschland*", reoccupied Belgorod.

The III and XL Panzer Corps of the 1st *Panzerarmee* mopped up the Debal'tsevo, Makeyevka, and Kramatorskaya pockets. The result of this drive was that the VII

Guards Cavalry Corps (Major-General Borisov), the IV Guards Mechanised Corps (Major-General Tanichikhin), and the XXV Tank Corps (Major-General Pavlov) found themselves trapped and then surrounded. The bridgehead at Matveyev-Kurgan, on the west bank of the Mius, was retaken by the 6th Army.

The spring thaw

About March 18, the thaw and the resultant mud caused operations to come to a halt between Kursk and the Sea of Azov. On that day, an O.K.W. communiqué proclaimed that Manstein's counter-attack had cost the enemy more than 50,000 killed, 19,594 prisoners, 3,000 guns, and 1,410 tanks. Without even questioning the figures, it is easy to put them into proportion by revealing that, in contrast, the Red Army had destroyed between 40 and 45 German and satellite divisions – a quarter of the forces the Russians had before them – in four months.

Dönitz takes over

On the morning of December 31, 1942 an engagement took place in the Barents Sea which had no important strategic consequences, but should be mentioned as it provoked a crisis in the German high command. The occasion was the passage off the North Cape in Norway of convoy J.W. 51B; its 14 merchant ships and tankers were taking 2,040 trucks, 202 tanks, 87 fighters, 43 bombers, 20,120 tons of oil fuel, 12,650 tons of petrol, and 54,321 tons of various products to Murmansk.

This large convoy was escorted by a minesweeper, two trawlers, two corvettes, and six destroyers (shortly reduced to five, as one had to give up after its gyroscopic compass had broken down). The small escort was commanded by Captain Robert St. V. Sherbrooke, a direct descendant of the famous Admiral Jervis who became Lord St. Vincent after his victory in 1797 over the Spanish fleet. Under the command of Rear-Admiral R. L. Burnett, a veteran of the Arctic run, the cruisers *Sheffield* and *Jamaica*, which were escorting a Murmansk con-

voy back to England, were in a position to protect it in case of an unlucky encounter. Lastly, nine submarines (including the Polish *Sokol* and the Dutch *O 14*) provided a protective screen for the convoy as it passed the Norwegian coast. Moreover, because of the winter ice floes the convoy J.W. 51B was sailing in single file about 240 miles from the German base at Altenfjord and its position had been signalled to Grand-Admiral Raeder by the *U-354* (Lieutenant Herschleb). Raeder acted very quickly on receiving this signal, as Hitler had recently made some extremely unflattering remarks about the Kriegsmarine. Therefore on that same evening of December 30, the pocket battleship *Lützow,* the heavy cruiser *Admiral Hipper,* and six destroyers put out to sea to intercept and destroy the convoy the following dawn. For this purpose, Vice-Admiral Kummetz, who was in command at sea, sent off his two major units in a pincer movement. But as he weighed anchor, he received a message from Admiral Kübler, the commander of the northern sector, which was clearly not

△ The occasional failure to heed such warnings sometimes cost the Allies very dear: Convoy S.C. 118 suffered heavily at the beginning of February because a captive could not keep his mouth shut.
▽ The unmistakable sign of a blazing tanker—a thick, black column of smoke, drawing U-boats to the convoy like ants to honey.

△ *The British destroyer* Orwell, *sister ship of Sherbrooke's* Onslow *and one of the four "O"-class destroyers involved in the Battle of the Barents Sea. The ships of this class were all launched in 1941 and 1942, and had a displacement of 1,540 tons, an armament of four 4.7-inch guns and eight 21-inch torpedo tubes, and a speed of 36¾ knots. The class was designed with quick conversion into minelayers in mind, and four of the eight eventually underwent the conversion.*

calculated to spur him on:

"Contrary to the operational order regarding contact against the enemy [you are] to use caution even against enemy of equal strength because it is undesirable for the cruisers to take any great risks."

Here Kübler was merely repeating the instructions sent to him by the chief of the *Oberkommando der Kriegsmarine* through Kiel and Admiral Carls. But Raeder was following a standing order promulgated by the Führer after the sinking of the *Bismarck,* and that evening Vice-Admiral Krancke, who had informed Hitler that the two ships and their escort vessels had sailed, wrote:

"The Führer emphasised that he wished to have all reports immediately since, as I well knew, he could not sleep a wink when ships were operating.

"I passed this message subsequently to the Operations Division of the Naval Staff, requesting that any information be telephoned immediately."

Hitler's anxiety was certainly peculiar, since he did not lose any sleep over the terrible fate of the 230,000 Germans encircled in the Stalingrad pocket.

On the next day, at about 0915, Kummetz, who had chosen *Hipper* as his

flagship, came into contact with the rear of the convoy. But *Onslow* (Captain Sherbrooke) fearlessly attacked the Germans, followed by three other destroyers. Meanwhile a fifth destroyer, which was under enemy fire, covered the merchant ships withdrawing towards the south-east under a smokescreen. In spite of his impressive superiority in guns, the German admiral did not dare to launch a full-scale attack, as he was afraid that in the prevailing half-light he would not be able to defend himself against the torpedoes which the British would certainly use against him if he came within range. At 1019 the first 8-inch shell hit *Onslow*, three more hits followed, killing 14 men and wounding 33, including Captain Sherbrooke, who lost an eye and had his nose fractured, but continued leading his division.

Lützow appeared a little later and tried to attack the convoy from the rear whilst *Hipper* engaged the escort vessels; however, as visibility was poor and her commander too unenterprising, her six 11- and eight 6-inch guns were hardly fired once. At 1130, the balance of the engagement changed; Rear-Admiral Burnett, who had been alerted by Sherbrooke, appeared on the scene just at the ight time; as he was north of *Hipper*, he was able to take advantage of the light to the south while remaining in the darkness himself. Moreover *Sheffield* and *Jamaica*, which both remained unscathed, scored three hits on the German flagship, which retreated with a boiler room flooded with a mixture of sea water and oil fuel.

We shall not describe the game of blind man's buff that followed; during the engagement, the destroyer *Friedrich Eckholdt* was sunk by the British cruisers, which she took for *Lützow* and *Hipper*. *Lützow* fired 86 11-inch and 76 6-inch shells, but none of them scored a direct hit. When the darkness increased, Kummetz broke off contact and the convoy set off again, reaching Murmansk without further mishap. Apart from the damage done to *Onslow*, the convoy had also lost the minesweeper *Bramble* and the destroyer *Achates*, which had heroically sacrificed herself in protecting the front of the convoy.

Hitler's adverse opinion

At Rastenburg, Hitler was awaiting news of the engagement with feverish impatience. At 1145 a message from *U-354* was intercepted and this appeared to indicate a major success; then, a few minutes later, came Kummetz's order to abandon the operation. But on his return journey Kummetz quite properly observed radio silence, and when he had anchored in the Altenfjord a whole series of fortuitous incidents combined to delay the transmission of his report, with the result that at 1700 on January 1 the Führer had nothing but the British communiqué to hand concerning the previous day's engagement. He violently upbraided Admiral Krancke:

"He said that it was an unheard of impudence not to inform him; and that such behaviour and the entire action showed that the ships were utterly useless; that they were nothing but a breeding ground for revolution, idly lying about and lacking any desire to get into action.

"This meant the passing of the High Seas Fleet, he said, adding that it was now his irrevocable decision to do away with these useless ships. He would put the good personnel, the good weapons, and the armour plating to better use."

He received Kummetz's report a few hours later, but it failed to placate him. Far from it, for according to Krancke:

"There was another outburst of anger with special reference to the fact that the action had not been fought to the finish. This, said the Führer, was typical of German ships, just the opposite of the British, who, true to their tradition, fought to the bitter end.

"If an English commander behaved like that he would immediately be relieved of his command. The whole thing spelled the end of the German High Seas Fleet, he declared. I was to inform the Grand-Admiral immediately that he was to come to the Führer at once, so that he could be informed personally of this irrevocable decision."

He added: "I am not an obliging civilian, but the commander-in-chief of all the armed forces."

In this long diatribe, the argument that Vice-Admiral Kummetz had not pursued the engagement to its conclusion was perfectly correct. But it was hardly seemly for Krancke to call Hitler to account for the paralysing effect that his orders had had on the movements of the

▽ Onslow *arrives home after her ordeal. She had been hit by four 8-inch shells from* Hipper, *and these had knocked out her two forward guns, killed 14 of her crew, and severely wounded her commander, Captain Sherbrooke.*

On August 27, 1941, the Type VIIC U-570 was captured and impressed as the British Graph.
▲ The German crew huddle on the conning tower under the guns of one of the aircraft that kept them covered until a Royal Navy prize crew arrived.
▷▷ Naval officers arrive in a Carley float to take possession.
▷ The prize arrives in Britain.
▽ Graph (far right) alongside the depôt ship Forth in June 1943.
▷▷▷ The end of a tanker.

fleet on that occasion. Grand-Admiral Raeder arrived at Rastenburg on January 6, 1943 and was immediately faced with an indictment which began with the part played by the Royal Prussian Navy in the war over the Duchies of Schleswig and Holstein (1864) and went on for over 90 minutes; Hitler's tone was bitterly hostile throughout and he used arguments which, according to Raeder, were so incompetent that they seemed to show the influence of *Reichsmarschall* Hermann Göring.

"Battleships," raged Hitler, "to which he had always devoted his full attention and which had filled him with so much pride were no longer of the slightest use. They required the permanent protection of planes and small ships. In the event of an Allied attack on Norway, these planes would be more usefully employed against the invasion fleet than protecting our own fleet. Large battleships no longer served any purpose and therefore must be taken out of commission, after their guns had been removed. There was an urgent need for their guns on land."

Raeder was, however, authorised to submit to Hitler a memo expressing his objections. Feeling himself offended and discredited by Hitler's manner of address-

ing him, Raeder, who was over 66 years old, asked for and obtained his retirement. On January 30, 1943 he therefore gave up the high command he had held for 15 years and took over an honorary inspectorate-general. But before handing over the command of the German Navy to Admiral Dönitz, he regarded it as his duty to inform the Führer of the disagreeable but inevitable consequences of discarding the Grand Fleet.

The Royal Navy would obtain at no cost to themselves the equivalent of a great naval victory. But even more important, Hitler had overlooked the fact that the application of his "irrevocable decision" would perceptibly affect the balance of forces in the Mediterranean, the Indian Ocean, and the Pacific. In fact, as soon as the potential threat of the German major warships in the North Atlantic disappeared, the Admiralty, recovering full freedom of action, would profit by it and crush Japan.

Events showed that Raeder saw clearly. It is known now that Churchill was impatiently waiting for the time when the elimination of German surface warships would allow the Navy to appear in the Far East again; he was determined to

Captain F. Walker, Britain's most prolific U-boat killer. He was born in 1896, and at the beginning of the war was head of the experimental department at the Navy's anti-submarine school. Late in 1941 he was given command of the sloop *Stork* and the 36th Group, with which he sank seven U-boats between December 1941 and June 1942. After a spell on shore, he returned to sea in the sloop *Starling* as commander of the famous 2nd Escort Group. He died on board his ship on July 9, 1944 and was buried at sea.

Fleet, thus giving it a wide margin of superiority in any circumstance. Thus when the powerful *Richelieu* had been refitted and sailed from Brooklyn dockyard, the Admiralty ensured that in November 1943 she joined the other ships at Scapa Flow.

Although he was a U-boat officer, the new Grand-Admiral deferred to the arguments of his predecessor, and Hitler was hardly in a position to thwart him immediately after his appointment.

In these circumstances, by a decision taken on February 18, 1943, the old battleships *Schlesien* and *Schleswig-Holstein,* which had been launched in 1906, the heavy cruiser *Admiral Hipper,* and the light cruisers *Köln* and *Leipzig* were merely declared obsolete, and the radical measures advocated by Hitler were not carried out. In fact, even this decision was only partially carried out; in autumn 1944 some of these units were to appear again in the Baltic to give gunfire support to Army Group "North" in its defence of the Kurland bridgehead.

Captain Sherbrooke had the exceptional distinction of winning the Victoria Cross for his exploit in the Barents Sea.

△ *The ex-Admiralty yacht* Enchantress *takes on supplies at sea. Note the lattice-work H/F D/F mast on the quarterdeck, which allowed German U-boat radio transmissions to be picked up and plotted.*
▽ *The depth charge crew of an armed trawler in action. The desperate shortage of inshore escort craft dictated that many hundreds of trawlers be converted to undertake this vital war work.*

restore British prestige there, impaired as it had been by the loss of Singapore; and Churchill doubtless had no wish to concede the monopoly of victory over Japan to the Americans, as he was well aware of the fanatical anti-colonialism displayed by Roosevelt. Hitler's whim, if it had been acted upon, would therefore have benefited only the Allies. This is shown by the fact that the Admiralty had to attach a force of battleships and aircraft-carriers to the Home

The *guerre de course*

"The balance sheet of profit and loss in mercantile tonnage was one of the most disturbing issues which confronted the Casablanca Conference when it opened on the 14th of January 1943. Until the U-boats were defeated the offensive strategy to which the Allies were committed could not succeed. Europe could never be invaded until the battle of the Atlantic had been won, and the latter purpose had therefore to be made a first charge on all Allied resources."

Thus Samuel W. Roskill, the Royal Navy's official historian, begins his chapter describing the decisive phase of this merciless struggle, and one can only confirm his judgement. There is no doubt that even after this battle had been won, the Western Allies would still have gained nothing until the European continent had been invaded, but if this first battle had been lost, all would have been lost with it.

When he took over the command of the German Navy, Karl Dönitz probably made no attempt to disown responsibility for the battle of the Atlantic; he knew what was at stake better than anyone else on the German side. Therefore the new commander-in-chief of U-boats, Rear-Admiral Godt, whom Dönitz himself selected, became even more closely subordinate to the latter's authority than the latter himself had previously been to Raeder. Consequently Dönitz was responsible for all the successes and defeats in this campaign, both before and after his promotion to the command of the Kriegsmarine, though one must make allowances for the fact that he was never free of Hitler's interference.

On January 1, 1943, the German Navy had 212 operational submarines, more than double its strength compared with the same date in 1942, when it had 91. In addition it had another 181 in the Baltic, either training or on trials. Moreover, the Third Reich's shipyards produced 23 or 24 submarines a month in 1943, in spite of Anglo-American bombing. However, as they lacked crews, the U-boats stayed longer and longer in the dockyards when they returned from their cruises; at the end of 1942 they averaged two months in dock to 40 days at sea.

At the beginning of 1943, in this decisive year, the 212 operational submarines

were distributed as follows:

Atlantic: 164
Mediterranean: 24
North Sea: 21
Black Sea: 3, moving down the Danube from Ratisbon.

In the main theatre of operations, 98 units were at sea at this time. However, 59 of them were in transit. These were forbidden to attack when they left harbour, unless in exceptional circumstances, and they very often had no torpedoes on the way back. They still used pack tactics, and the strength of their packs had doubled and even tripled since the beginning of 1942. In February and March 1943 there were sometimes 10, 12, or even 16 submarines attacking the same convoy for days on end. Their effectiveness was much strengthened by the fact that German Naval Counter-Intelligence managed continually to decipher Allied communications. "Thus we obtained," Admiral Dönitz wrote at this time, "not only information about the convoys but also, in January and February 1943, the 'U-boat positions', communicated from time to time by the British Admiralty to the commanders of convoys at sea to show them the confirmed or conjectured positions of our warships

△ △ *Impromptu conference in the North Atlantic between two U-boats. With the gradual closing of the "Atlantic gap" and the strengthening of Allied escort for convoys, it was now becoming very dangerous for U-boats to stay on the surface in daylight and also to communicate with each other or with headquarters by radio.*
△ *The U-boat pens at Lorient. Quite wrongly the R.A.F. had decided to attack these only when they were finished – which proved to be a fruitless task as their concrete construction made them impregnable.*

in their sector. This was extremely valuable, as we often asked ourselves what the enemy knew about us.''

Even today, it is hard to explain the reasons why Dönitz was allowed to read, so to speak, over his enemy's shoulder; the British in fact knew nothing of this for three years and never took the appropriate counter-measures.

When they returned from their cruises,

the U-boats were sheltered in the concrete pens at Lorient and la Pallice from December 1941, and later at Brest, St. Nazaire, and Bordeaux; the pens' 22-foot thick roofs were capable of withstanding the heaviest bombs. As has been mentioned, the R.A.F. did not attack them while they were being built, and when it did so, in accordance with a decision taken at Casablanca, it had no military result. From January to May 1943 English and American bombers dropped about 8,000 tons of bombs and incendiaries on the German Atlantic bases, all to no effect; in vain they destroyed Brest, Lorient, and St. Nazaire without obtaining a single hit on their real targets. The only U-boat sunk at anchor was *U-622*, which was destroyed at Trondheim by a U.S. plane on July 24, 1943. And whilst the French population suffered very severely in these badly directed operations, they cost the Allies 98 planes. One final point: it appears that Raeder's successor was now reduced to using anything that came to hand for sustaining the enormous effort of the submarine war. Unquestionably, his fleets became more and more accident-prone. There were three in 1942 and nine in the following year, seven of them training in the Baltic.

Moreover, the new Grand Admiral had to withstand the weight of this campaign alone. He could not expect any assistance from the Luftwaffe. In fact, during 1943 R.A.F. patrols sank 41 U-boats in the Bay of Biscay without any serious interference from the Germans. It is not surprising that Dönitz, exasperated by the frequent criticisms of the German Navy continually made by Hermann Göring to Hitler, permitted himself a tart reply: "Herr *Reichsmarschall*, kindly spare me your criticisms of the Kriegsmarine. You have got quite enough to do looking after the Luftwaffe!"

Stepped-up production

We shall now consider the Allies' defence against the U-boats.

During 1943 the Western powers' anti-U-boat weapons production was sufficient to meet the extent and urgency of the threat, but the Allied effort was not as one-sided as the Germans', as it placed more importance on the aerial side of naval warfare. However, one must have many reservations about the use the British and Americans made of their air forces in their campaign against the U-boats.

This effort was from now on mainly American. Admittedly, the tactics and technology were mostly British, but the mass production needed to get them into action was predominantly American. The difference in industrial power between the two countries was enormous; the United States, moreover, which had suffered neither Blitz nor black-out, made tremendous innovations in prefabrication.

Escort craft

Amongst escort ships, the British frigate corresponded in its general features to the escort destroyer of the U.S. Navy. But from 1943 till the end of hostilities, Great Britain, with the help of Canadian dockyards, produced 100 frigates, whilst the Americans in the same space of time built 565 escort destroyers; 78 of these were handed over to Britain under Lend-Lease, while eight went to Brazil and six

△ Admiral Karl Dönitz, who was now promoted to the command of the whole Kriegsmarine with the rank of Grand-Admiral. From here on the desperate struggle against Allied naval and merchant marine strength would be in the hands of this one capable man. He had, however, not only to contend with rapidly increasing Allied strength, but also with Hitler's whimsical idiosyncrasies and Göring's destructive inefficiency.
◁ The raw stuff of Germany's naval struggle. Despite the increasingly heavy losses now suffered by the U-boat service, Dönitz was never short of volunteers for his submarine crews.

It was as if some outside agency had suddenly decided to take a hand on the Allied side—all of a sudden U-boat losses started to climb considerably, while merchant shipping losses declined at an even faster rate. The crisis had been reached and passed, and although the Germans continued their offensive with all the means at their disposal, the Allies had weathered this critical point in their fortunes.

△ A stricken U-boat begins to founder amid a welter of spray.

◁ ◁ A U-boat crew abandons ship just before its vessel is sent to the bottom by one U.S. Navy and two U.S. Coast Guard destroyer escorts. One of the Coast Guard vessels picked up 12 survivors.

◁△ Another U-boat begins to sink by the stern as its crew scrambles off the conning tower. Note the plumes of water off the U-boat's starboard beam, thrown up by machine gun fire from the Sunderland flying boat responsible for the "kill".

◁▽ U-boat survivors in a string of one-man dinghies.

to France. These ships were a little faster than the corvettes of 1940; they had considerable freedom of movement and were profusely armed and equipped for their specialised rôle.

Escort carriers

The story of escort carriers is similar. The British had commissioned their first such carrier, *Audacity,* in November 1941; she was sunk on December 21, 1941, but had performed such signal services that the Admiralty decided to build half a dozen similar ships. The British could not produce as many as the Americans, however, who built 115 between the summer of 1942 and the capitulation of Japan, on new hulls or by converting cargo ships or tankers. But again these 7,000 to 12,000 ton ships were produced quickly and promptly by the prefabrication methods previously referred to. One may take as examples the aircraft carriers *Bogue, Card,* and *Core:*

	Laid down	Launched	Commissioned
Bogue	October 1, 1941	January 15, 1942	September 26, 1942
Card	October 27, 1941	February 21, 1942	November 8, 1942
Core	January 2, 1942	May 15, 1942	December 10, 1942

Considering their escort rôle, a speed of not more than 20 knots was acceptable for carriers of this type. As a result of this feature and the restricted length of their flight decks, catapults had to be installed to launch the planes, of which there were about 20 (fighters and torpedo-bombers). In addition, escort carriers were employed in landing operations as aircraft transports, and as tankers; as they served so many purposes and in such large numbers, they were nicknamed "Woolworth carriers".

By July 1943, the American fleet already had 29 escort carriers in service. Their usefulness soon became evident: by December 31 in the same year they had already destroyed 26 U-boats, and the *Card* alone had accounted for eight of these. Thirty-eight of the 115 escort carriers built by the Americans fought under the British flag.

Operational research

Owing to the increase in the number of escort ships, the convoys were now reinforced; later, "support groups" were also formed as a strategic reserve. The work of the Department of Operational Studies facilitated this development; it was initiated by the Admiralty under the direction of P. M. S. Blackett, professor of physics at Manchester University and Nobel prizewinner in 1948. This organisation also made a most important deduction concerning merchant ship losses; as Captain Macintyre puts it:

"Whereas the number of ships lost in a convoy battle depended, as might be expected, upon the number of U-boats attacking and the size of the escort, it was quite independent of the size of the convoy."

When he demonstrated that the number of escort ships was being built up much more slowly than that of the ships to be escorted, Professor Blackett proved thereby, and in the face of most people's idea of common sense, that large convoys were proportionately less vulnerable than small ones. An important conclusion followed. Macintyre puts it thus:

"Then, as has been said, the economy of force, achieved by reducing the number of convoys to be defended, provided a surplus of warships which could be formed into Support Groups. These themselves resulted in a further economy. For, provided that the convoy escort could be reinforced during the passage of the most dangerous areas, a smaller escort could safely be given for the remainder of the convoy's voyage. Thus Operational Research, too often neglected or ignored, was responsible for a revolution in organisation, which came about in March 1943 with an adjustment of the North Atlantic convoy cycle, whereby fewer and larger convoys were sailed each way."

To the best of our knowledge, this was the first application of what is today called operational research, which is now essential, with the aid of computers, not only in military operations but also in sociology, economics, industry, and commerce.

As regards anti-submarine equipment, we may mention that centimetric wavelength radar equipment was installed on Allied ships and planes; its pulses could not be picked up by the detection apparatus installed by German engineers on all U-boats. In July, however, an R.A.F. bomber carrying this most modern radar equipment was brought down over Rotterdam. Grand-Admiral Dönitz thus learned the secret of the defeat he had suffered, but it was now too late.

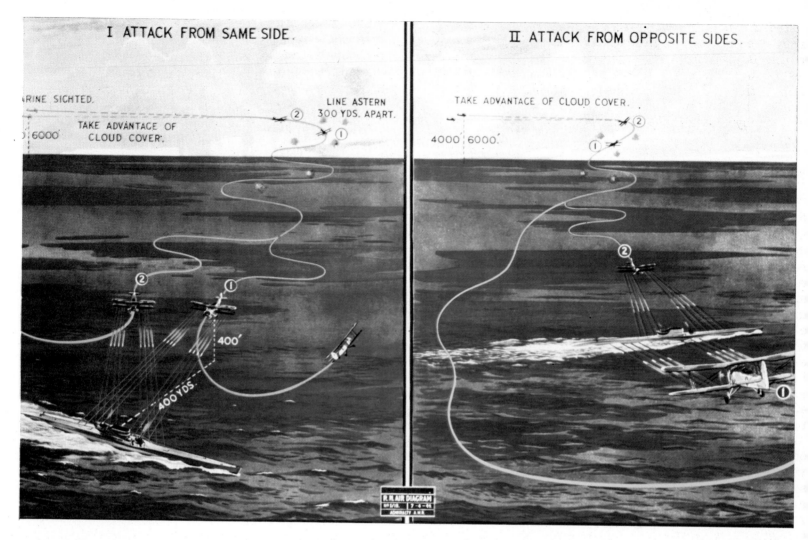

I ATTACK FROM SAME SIDE.

II ATTACK FROM OPPOSITE SIDES.

△ *Yet another rôle for the obsolescent but still versatile Fairey Swordfish: anti-submarine rocket operations. With their docile handling characteristics and low landing speed, these aircraft were ideal for operation from the new escort carriers. From now to the end of the war, large numbers of U-boats were fated to fall to the aircraft of these carriers, both British and American.*

"Huff Duff" . . .

H/F D/F (High Frequency Direction Finder), goniometric radio equipment, nicknamed "Huff Duff", was undoubtedly another factor in the Allies' success in the Battle of the Atlantic. This had the capacity to detect U-boats whenever they were compelled to transmit. Thus the convoy could be directed away from the area where a pack of submarines was gathering, and a support group of "Hunter-Killers", as the Americans called them, could be launched against them. The U.S. Navy and Army Air Force ordered no less than 3,200 sets of this equipment.

. . . and "Hedgehog"

At the beginning of 1943, the "Hedgehog" was put into general use. This was a projector, fitted in the bows of an escort vessel, which fired a pattern of 24 contact-fused bombs to a range of 250 yards. Thus the pursuer did not have to pass vertically over the top of the submerged target before firing its depth charges.

Finally the rockets which were successfully used by Montgomery's fighter-bombers against the Panzers were also used with the same redoubtable efficiency against the U-boats by the R.A.F.'s, U.S.A.A.F.'s, and U.S.N.'s anti-submarine patrol aircraft.

On May 23, 1942 the new weapon was first used with success by a Swordfish from the British escort carrier *Archer*. In his excellent book on fleet air arm warfare Admiral Barjot gives the following description:

"On the morning of May 23, the convoy was in sight off Newfoundland and the first wave started to attack. The Swordfish B 819 then took off and almost immediately had the good fortune to surprise *U-572,* which had surfaced to keep up with the convoy. The eight rockets lanced off towards the U-boat, holing it so that it had to surface again quickly, as its batteries were flooded. It tried to use its guns, but the fight only lasted a few minutes. A Martlet fighter arrived and machine gunned the U-boat, killing its captain and several men. The rest of the crew lost hope and abandoned ship, the U-boat sinking almost immediately. A few Germans were picked up later by the destroyer *Escapade*."

Bomber Command's part

Following a decision at the Casablanca Conference, the R.A.F.'s Bomber Command and the bomber groups of the American 8th Air Force in England redoubled their attacks against the German shipyards where submarines were under construction. Thus it was hoped to eliminate the danger at its source. In fact, according to Roskill, between May 1 and June 1 the British and American heavy squadrons carried out 3,414 sorties and dropped 5,572 tons of bombs and 4,173 of incendiaries on these targets, now recognised as of prime importance.

But in spite of the loss of 168 planes, the efforts were virtually fruitless. Even worse, this air offensive, which had been so warmly recommended by Churchill and Roosevelt, frustrated the British and American effort in the Atlantic; Bomber Command's requests for reinforcements and replacements could in fact only be satisfied if a parsimonious policy was maintained towards Coastal Command, at least as regards long-range four-engined aircraft for convoy protection.

Professor Blackett realised this perfectly clearly. In 1943 he extended his criticism to all R.A.F. Bomber Command operations:

"From the figures on the effectiveness of air cover, it could be calculated that a long-range Liberator operating from Iceland and escorting the convoys in the middle of the Atlantic *saved* at least half a dozen merchant ships in its service life-time of some thirty flying sorties. If used for bombing Berlin, the same aircraft in its service life would drop less than 100 tons of bombs and kill not more than a couple of dozen enemy men, women and children and destroy a number of houses.

"No one would dispute that the saving of six merchant ships and their crews and cargoes was of incomparably more value to the Allied war effort than the killing of some two dozen enemy civilians, the destruction of a number of houses and a certain very small effect on production.

"The difficulty was to get the figures believed. But believed they eventually were and more long-range aircraft were made available to Coastal Command."

In fact in February 1943, Air-Marshal Sir John Slessor, who succeeded Sir Philip Joubert de la Ferté as head of Coastal Command, had only ten four-engined B-24 Liberators, whilst the American Navy had only 52. On July 1, however, the figures had risen to 37 and 209 respectively.

▽ *The commander of a German U-boat weighs up the situation before deciding whether or not to make an attack.*
▽▽ *While the captain makes his decision, the torpedo-room crew complete their final preparations on the weapons in the tubes and on the reloads.*

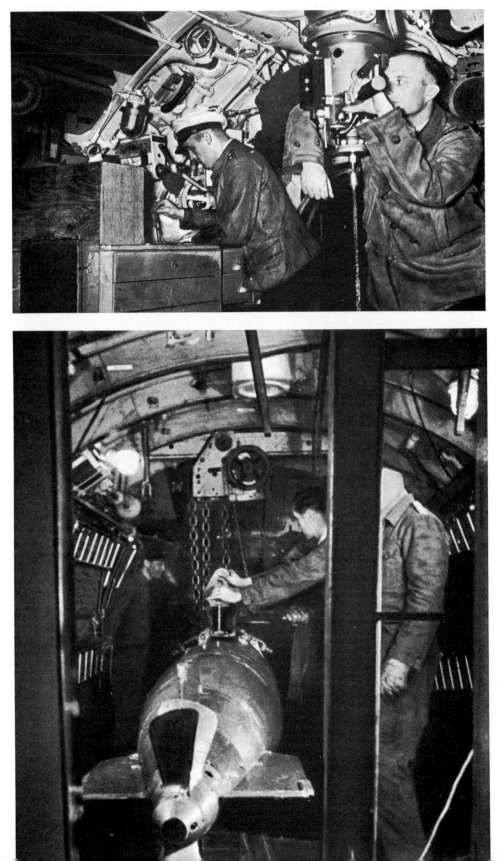

a careless word...

A NEEDLESS LOSS

CHAPTER 90
Defeat of the U-boats

The graph below gives a precise account of the changing fortunes of the Battle of the Atlantic in 1943, and little more comment is needed. As can be seen, January was relatively favourable to the Allies, as winter storms raged over the North Atlantic; in fact they only lost 50 merchant vessels (261,359 tons) against 106 (419,907 tons) in the same month of the previous year.

West of the Canaries, however, a pack of eight submarines skilfully directed to its rendezvous by Dönitz attacked a convoy of nine tankers heading for North Africa; seven of these were sunk; this was a remarkable feat for which Dönitz duly received General von Arnim's congratulations. In February, Allied losses increased and were slightly over 400,000 tons (73 ships). Nonetheless, between the 4th and 9th of this month, the slow convoy S.C. 118 (63 merchantmen and ten escort vessels) fought off 20 U-boats for four successive nights. A survivor from a previous attack, picked up by *U-632*, had been criminally indiscreet and drawn the attention of his captors to the convoy: the survivor's remarks caused the loss of several hundreds of his comrades' lives. In fact 13 cargo-boats were sunk at dawn on February 9, but as Grand-Admiral

Dönitz stated, the defence was keen: "It was", he wrote, "perhaps the worst battle of the whole submarine war. Honour to the crews and commanders who waged it in the harsh winter conditions of the Atlantic! It went on for four successive nights, and the captains were unable to leave their bridges for the whole period. Their ships' safety often depended on the speed of their decisions. It is hard to imagine the self-discipline that is required after a terrible depth-charge attack, to give orders to surface, to approach the convoy, and to bear down on it through its protective screen, bristling with steel, with the alternative of success or destruction. The submarine commanders never performed such a colossal feat in the course of both world wars."

This opinion can be confirmed. The loss of the 13 cargo vessels previously mentioned was countered by that of three U-boats sunk by the escort vessels. They included *U-609* (Lieutenant Rudloff) which was sunk by a depth charge from the French corvette *Lobelia* (Lieutenant de Morsier). In other engagements, a further 16 U-boats were lost during February; on February 28, for the first time since hostilities began, the number of U-boats lost almost equalled the number

▽ *Evidence that the threat of the U-boat was finally beaten: merchant shipping losses falling, U-boat losses rising.*

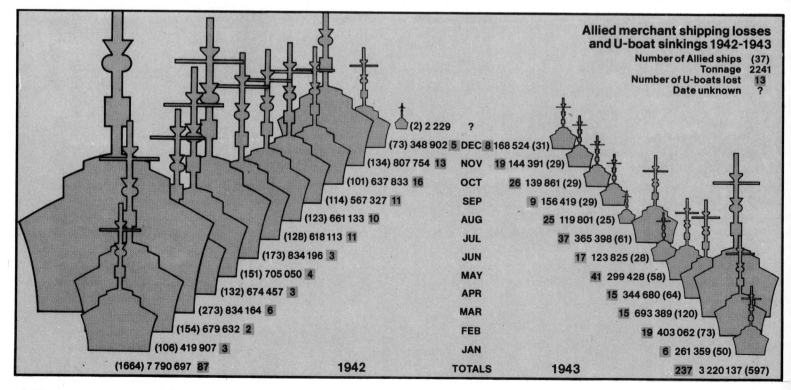

Allied merchant shipping losses and U-boat sinkings 1942-1943

Number of Allied ships	(37)
Tonnage	2241
Number of U-boats lost	13
Date unknown	?

1942			MONTH		1943	
(2)	2 229	?				
(73)	348 902	5	DEC	8	168 524	(31)
(134)	807 754	13	NOV	19	144 391	(29)
(101)	637 833	16	OCT	26	139 861	(29)
(114)	567 327	11	SEP	9	156 419	(29)
(123)	661 133	10	AUG	25	119 801	(25)
(128)	618 113	11	JUL	37	365 398	(61)
(173)	834 196	3	JUN	17	123 825	(28)
(151)	705 050	4	MAY	41	299 428	(58)
(132)	674 457	3	APR	15	344 680	(64)
(273)	834 164	6	MAR	15	693 389	(120)
(154)	679 632	2	FEB	19	403 062	(73)
(106)	419 907	3	JAN	6	261 359	(50)
(1664)	7 790 697	87	TOTALS	237	3 220 137	(597)

completed by German yards.

In view of this slaughter and the escape, which was often noted, of the convoys from the U-boat onslaught, Dönitz thought for a time that a spy or even a traitor must have penetrated his own staff. The *Abwehr* conducted a search to locate him, but without success. This was not surprising, as, when they changed course to avoid packs, the British and the Americans relied on the contact signals transmitted by their opponents and picked up by their Huff Duff devices. Huff Duff operators had now had so much experience that they were no longer content only to spy out the enemy, but as they were personally involved in operating the device, they also often managed to identify him. In fact the Kriegsmarine only got to the bottom of the mystery at the end of the war. In 1956 the official historian of the Royal Navy came to the following conclusion about the sea engagements of March 1943:

"Nor can one yet look back on that month without feeling something approaching horror over the losses we suffered. In the first ten days, in all waters, we lost forty-one ships; in the second ten days fifty-six. More than half a million tons of shipping was sunk in those twenty days; and, what made the losses so much more serious than the bare figures can indicate, was that nearly two-thirds of the ships sunk during the month were in convoy."

Had the system of convoys, begun in September 1939, outlived its usefulness? This was the question which the Admiralty was now anxiously debating. Captain Roskill quotes the following comment from one of its reports, drawn up at the end of 1943:

"The Germans never came so near to disrupting communications between the New World and the Old as in the first

△ *Part of the team that beat Dönitz's U-boats. Seen at Coastal Command's headquarters at Northwood in Middlesex are Air-Marshal Sir John Slessor, Commander-in-Chief of Coastal Command (centre), Air Vice-Marshal A. Durston, Slessor's Senior Air Staff Officer (left), and Captain D. V. Peyton-Ward, Slessor's Senior Naval Staff Officer (right). Behind them a W.A.A.F. is plotting movements on a large wall map. According to Slessor, the Bay of Biscay was "the trunk of the Atlantic U-boat menace", and in this area Coastal Command sank 25 U-boats between April and August 1943.*

△ U-boat eye view of a sinking merchantman. Note the marks of the periscope graticule, which helped the commander gauge the range and speed of the target for incorporation into the calculations made on the plotting table. This gave the captain information as to when and where to fire his torpedoes, plus the best speed and depth to set them to run.

twenty days of March 1943."

Between March 7 and 11, the slow convoy S.C. 121 lost 13 of its ships, and these losses remained unavenged. The submarines were not so lucky when they engaged the fast convoy H.X. 228; four merchant ships were destroyed at the cost of two U-boats. During this engagement, according to Captain Macintyre, the commander of the cargo vessel *Kingswood* almost rammed a German U-boat:

"In the darkness and the gale, as he peered anxiously out from his bridge, his eye was caught by what seemed to be a particularly heavy breaking sea on his port bow. Then he saw that the white flurry was travelling with some speed towards him. 'It's a torpedo,' he shouted to the mate standing beside him. But almost at once he realised that he was in fact looking at the wash of a submarine travelling at high speed on the surface. He ran to the telegraph and gave a double ring, calling for the utmost emergency speed and steered to ram. 'I really felt we could not miss,' he recorded.

"'Collision seemed inevitable. About this time I heard the U-boat's engine and a voice in the distance. I was sort of hanging on waiting for the crash when I saw the submarine's wake curling round–the voice I heard must have been the U-boat's commander shouting "Hard a Port" in German. The submarine's wake curled right under my stem–how its tail missed us I still do not know.'"

On March 11, the destroyer *Harvester*

(Commander A. Tait) rammed *U-444* (Sub-Lieutenant Langfeld) which was then sunk by the French corvette *Aconit* (Lieutenant Levasseur). *Harvester,* however, had her propellers badly damaged and became an easy target for *U-432* (Lieutenant Eckhardt). When he saw the column of smoke that indicated *Harvester*'s end, Levasseur returned to the fray and managed to avenge Tait, who had gone down with his ship. From March 16 to 19, the battle reached its high point, pitting 38 submarines against the two convoys H.X. 229 and S.C. 122: in the three nights 21 cargo vessels were sunk whilst the attackers lost only one U-boat.

In all 120 merchant ships and tankers totalling 693,389 tons went down, including 82 (476,349 tons) in the North Atlantic, during March.

Dönitz's hopes were not encouraged by the events of April. Less than half the number of merchant ships were destroyed (344,680 tons), for the same number of submarines sunk (15). Moreover, the support groups and escort-carriers began to pursue the enemy more and more closely. The results were clear in May. In that month, at least 40 U-boats were destroyed: 28 were sunk in the North Atlantic, whilst Allied losses fell to below 300,000 tons.

"The situation was changing," wrote Dönitz, acknowledging defeat. "Radar, particularly in aircraft, virtually cancelled out the ability of our submarines to attack on the surface. The previous tactics of our submarines could now no longer be employed in the North Atlantic, a theatre where air reconnaissance was too strong for us. Before using such tactics again, we had to restore our submarines' fighting abilities. I drew my own conclusion and we evacuated the North Atlantic. On May 24 I ordered the submarines to rendezvous in the area south-west of the Azores, taking all the necessary precautions. We had lost the Battle of the Atlantic."

Captain Roskill warmly praises the British captains and crews and summarises the episode as follows:

"In its intensity, and in the certainty that its outcome would decide the issue of the war, the battle may be compared to the Battle of Britain of 1940. Just as Göring then tried with all the forces of the Luftwaffe to gain command of the skies over Britain, so now did Dönitz seek to gain command of the Atlantic

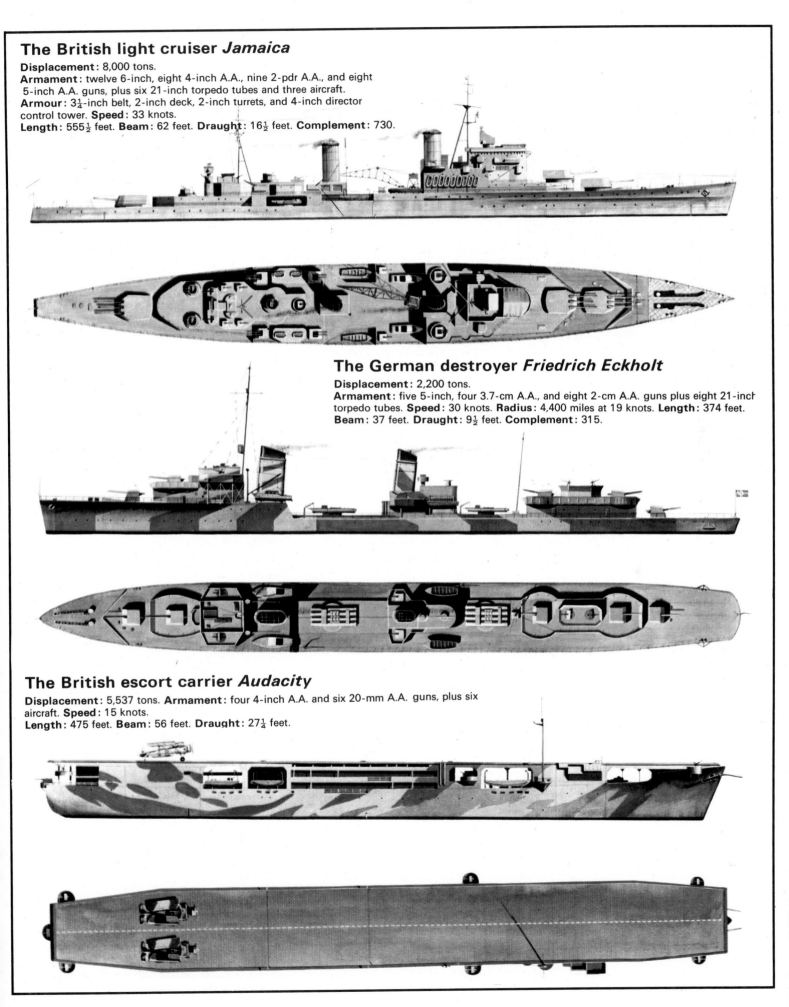

The British light cruiser *Jamaica*

Displacement: 8,000 tons.
Armament: twelve 6-inch, eight 4-inch A.A., nine 2-pdr A.A., and eight
5-inch A.A. guns, plus six 21-inch torpedo tubes and three aircraft.
Armour: 3¼-inch belt, 2-inch deck, 2-inch turrets, and 4-inch director
control tower. **Speed:** 33 knots.
Length: 555½ feet. **Beam:** 62 feet. **Draught:** 16½ feet. **Complement:** 730.

The German destroyer *Friedrich Eckholt*

Displacement: 2,200 tons.
Armament: five 5-inch, four 3.7-cm A.A., and eight 2-cm A.A. guns plus eight 21-inch
torpedo tubes. **Speed:** 30 knots. **Radius:** 4,400 miles at 19 knots. **Length:** 374 feet.
Beam: 37 feet. **Draught:** 9½ feet. **Complement:** 315.

The British escort carrier *Audacity*

Displacement: 5,537 tons. **Armament:** four 4-inch A.A. and six 20-mm A.A. guns, plus six
aircraft. **Speed:** 15 knots.
Length: 475 feet. **Beam:** 56 feet. **Draught:** 27¼ feet.

△ △ *A change at the head of the Home Fleet: Admiral Sir John Tovey (left) greets Vice-Admiral Sir Bruce Fraser on board his flagship as the latter takes over from him on May 8, 1943.*
△ *Rear-Admiral R. L. Burnett, who commanded the cruiser force in the action against* Hipper *and* Lützow *on December 31, 1942.*

with his U-boats. And the men who defeated him–the crews of the little ships, of the air escorts and of our tiny force of long-range aircraft–may justly be immortalised alongside 'the few' who won the 1940 battle of the air.''

Amongst these "few", Captain F. J. Walker's name should be mentioned; by March 14, 1944 his 2nd Escort Group had sunk 13 U-boats.

Dönitz shifts theatres

The first five months of 1943 had cost the Allies 365 ships (2,001,918 tons); in the following seven, the losses were reduced to 232 (1,218,219 tons). July was the only month in which the tonnage destroyed (365,398 tons) recalled the position in the first six months, but the Germans paid heavily for this.

Thirty-seven U-boats were lost, one per 10,000 tons sunk, whilst in March the proportion had been one to 46,200 tons.

As the British squadrons were reinforced by Coastal Command and supported by U.S. planes, they went over to the offensive in the Bay of Biscay. Dönitz thought he could ward off this threat by fitting quadruple 2-cm cannon on the conning towers of his U-boats. However, he was underestimating the danger of planes which were kept informed by radar and armed with heavy machine guns, rockets, bombs, and depth-charges. His failure to understand the situation cost him 22 U-boats between June 1 and September 1, 1943: he was therefore compelled to order his captains to submerge by day when they passed through these dangerous waters; thus their cruises took considerably longer. At night, when they recharged their batteries, his raiders still had to reckon with the enemy bombers, which were fitted with powerful radar-aimed Leigh searchlights.

In bringing the submarine war to the south-west of the Azores, the Grand-Admiral came up against the American defences.

At the Pentagon (which had just been built), Admiral Ernest J. King had appointed Rear-Admiral Francis Low as deputy chief-of-staff specially entrusted with anti-submarine problems. On receiving his report, King set up a 10th Fleet on the following May 20, which by his decision on that day ''was to exercise (under the direct command of COMINCH [C.-in-C.

U.S. Fleet]) unity of control over U.S. antisubmarine operations in that part of the Atlantic under U.S. strategic control.''

Low therefore only acted by King's delegation, whilst King retained command of the organisation. On the other hand, in contrast with what was happening on the other side of the Atlantic, where Sir Max Horton, C.-in-C. Western Approaches, had ships and marine aircraft, the 10th Fleet in Washington controlled neither boats nor planes. In the action it was directing, it therefore had to make use of the aircraft and formations of the Atlantic Fleet, to which it was not allowed to give any orders. This was the reason for what Ladislas Farago, the historian of the 10th Fleet, has called ''an impressive flowering of periphrases'' in its relations with Admiral Ingersoll, such as ''suggest that you...'', ''it is recommended that you...'', ''would it be possible for you to...?''

In spite of its paradoxical situation this organisation worked extremely efficiently from the beginning. In July and August the loss of 35 out of the 60 German submarines sunk in all theatres of war was undoubtedly due to the Americans. In the South Atlantic, where the U.S. 4th Fleet was operating, the groups centred on the escort carriers *Core, Santee, Card,* and *Bogue* (under the command respectively of Captains Greer, Fisk, Isbell, and Short) took a prominent and praiseworthy part in this success. The result was that in his commentary on this period of the merchant navy war, Admiral Dönitz wrote: ''Every zone in the South Atlantic was closely watched by long-range four-engined planes or by planes from American aircraft-carriers which were specially deployed to hunt submarines in the central and southern Atlantic. The same strict observation was practised even in the Indian Ocean, although not on such a wide scale. The planes of the two great naval powers therefore took a considerable part in the pursuit of our U-boats, and this continued till the end of hostilities.

''The situation was similar in more distant operational sectors.

''West of the Azores, our ships were still able in mid-June 1943 to refuel from a submarine tanker without interference, before operating in their sectors, which extended from the Straits of Florida to south of Rio de Janeiro and from Dakar to the interior of the Gulf of Guinea. Each

commander had a vast area in which to operate as circumstances permitted. We systematically avoided any concentration in order not to provoke a parallel defence concentration. At first the results were favourable, as 16 enemy vessels were sunk initially. But air observation increased rapidly and the boats, particularly those off the American coast, had difficulty in maintaining themselves in their sectors. Similarly, naval refuelling became so dangerous that we had to give it up, thus considerably shortening the length of operations."

Amongst the U-boats destroyed in this sector we may mention some returning from Penang in Malaya, which had valuable cargoes of rubber, tin, molybdenum, and tungsten.

The episodes of the submarine war are often moving, irrespective of one's sympathies. Ladislas Farago tells one story which may be found amusing. Lieutenant Johannsen's *U-569* had been put out of action by a plane from *Bogue:*

"Johannsen ordered his men to hoist the time-honoured symbol of surrender but the hapless submariners could not find anything white on the boat whose curtains, tablecovers and sheets were all made of some oil resistant drab green cloth. They waved what they had, but those improvised green surrender flags, whose colour blended with that of an angry sea, could not have been made out by Roberts who kept up his fire. However, they were spotted by the Canadian destroyer *St. Laurent* and such evident eagerness to surrender induced her skipper to make preparations for boarding the sub to capture. Johannsen's engineer officer spoiled the scheme. In the last moment he slipped below, opened the flood-valves and went down with the boat, leaving but twenty-four U-boat men for the *St. Laurent* to capture.

"Citing the U-Johannsen's fate, we recommended that the U-boats carry something white on board because our pilots could not be expected to distinguish any green cloth waved at them from the level of the green sea. Our suggestion was promptly heeded. A few weeks later the U-460 was in Johannsen's predicament. Its crew waved that 'something white' we had recommended to keep handy for such emergencies. The 'surrender flag' turned out to be the skipper's dress shirt."

On October 8, 1943 the agreement between the Portuguese and British

△ △ *The German battleship* Tirpitz *at anchor in Altenfjord. On the one side she was protected by the shore and on the other by anti-torpedo nets, with smoke projectors capable of covering the whole area in minutes well deployed all round this part of the fjord.*
△ *A British X-craft under way.*

△ *Waist gunners of a Sunderland flying boat. With the increase of Allied air strength over the Atlantic, U-boats were fitted with powerful A.A. defences. These in turn led to the fitting of a fixed forward firing battery of four machine guns on Sunderlands, to deal with the German A.A. crews.*
▽ *A quadruple 2-pdr "pom-pom" A.A. mounting on board a British warship.*

Governments granting the British naval and air forces the right to establish a base in the Azores was a new blow for German naval strategy; a few months later, moreover, the Americans were granted the same concession. Thus the "Atlantic gap" was finally closed.

The balance of losses

On December 31, 1943, the German submarine flotillas consisted of only 168 operational units; there had been 212 on the preceding January 1. During the year they had lost 237 U-boats and their crews. Eight of these were the result of accident, 75 were sunk by the Americans, five by the French, one by the Russians, and the remainder (148) by the Royal Navy and Coastal Command squadrons. As against these losses, we must put the losses of all kinds of Allied merchant vessels in 1943: they amounted to 3,220,137 tons, made up of 597 ships. These figures may appear very large, but they are nevertheless 4,570,000 tons and 1,067 ships less than the figures in 1942. During the same period merchant ships and tankers of about 13 million tons

were launched in British, Canadian, and American shipyards. Here again the predominance of the U.S.A. became apparent. Their Liberty ships, which were succeeded by their Victory ships, were built with prefabricated parts by methods recommended by the industrialist Henry Kayser, an organiser of genius; they played a distinguished part in the Allied victory of 1945 and the reconstruction of Western Europe, including Germany and Italy, after the close of hostilities. But in spite of this Dönitz did not give up. He believed that new arms would bring victory in 1944, and in the meantime he counted on forcing the enemy to squander his effort within the bounds of the Atlantic; otherwise the Allies would concentrate their resources even more against the industrial might of the Third Reich.

From January 1 to December 31, 1943, more than 680,000 Allied combatants were disembarked in Great Britain and Northern Ireland by 66 convoys as a part of Operation "Bolero", whilst about 127,000 left the British Isles for Africa, Sicily, and Italy. As a general rule the troops crossed the Atlantic without a convoy on fast liners which managed to elude U-boat ambushes. Using the "hot berth" system (two berths for three soldiers), the *Queen Elizabeth* and the *Queen Mary* transported 15,000 men per crossing, whilst the French ship *Pasteur* accommodated 4,500.

Nevertheless the rations, fighting equipment, vehicles, fuel, and ammunition for these 680,000 men went via the usual convoy route, and most of the bombers for the U.S. 8th Air Force and all the fighters reached Britain by sea. Even if they had crossed the Atlantic by air, or via Iceland, their fuel supply could only have been secured by the use of tankers. For this reason, we may conclude that if the German submarine raiders had not been defeated in 1943, there would have been no Second Front in Western Europe in 1944.

Operation "Bolero"

At the end of March 1943, the battle-cruiser *Scharnhorst* joined the battleship *Tirpitz* and pocket battleship *Lützow* at Trondheim, and then together the three reached Kåfjord, a small section of the Altenfjord about halfway between Tromsö and the North Cape. From this position they could harass the Allied convoys in the Arctic or even resume the war against the merchant ships in the Atlantic. As the Sicilian operations and the Salerno landing required six British warships in the Mediterranean, the Home Fleet, as whose commander Admiral Tovey had been succeeded by Sir Bruce Fraser in June 1943, had some difficulty in intercepting the German ships.

In addition, the Admiralty in London organised Operation "Source" under the command of Rear-Admiral C. B. Barry, Flag Officer Submarines. The purpose of this operation was to destroy this dangerous German force at anchor by using six 30-ton midget submarines; their armament consisted of two 2-ton charges which could be released to sink under the hull of the target, exploding when set off by a clockwork mechanism. A squadron of reconnaissance planes made Murmansk their base and gave the attackers all possible Intelligence about the obstacles and defences around the anchored German ships.

On September 11, six midget submarines (each manned by four men and towed by conventional submarines), left an unobtrusive harbour in the north of Scotland and sailed towards Altenfjord. One of them *(X-8)* was to attack *Lützow*, two *(X-9* and *X-10) Scharnhorst,* and the remaining three *(X-5, X-6,* and *X-7) Tirpitz.* But *X-9* was lost with all hands during the crossing, and *X-8* had to be scuttled because it was heavily damaged. The four remaining submarines suffered mishaps of all kinds; even if their compasses managed to work, their periscope tubes filled with water or the electrical engine used for raising them failed.

In spite of all this, at dawn on September 22 Lieutenants Cameron and Place managed to steer *X-6* and *X-7* below *Tirpitz* and release their charges. When *X-6* accidentally surfaced, the huge warship was alerted and had enough time to slew round at her anchorage, thereby managing to escape the worst. But two of her 15-inch gun turrets were immobilised and her engines were badly damaged, and she was out of action for several months. *X-5,* which followed *X-6* and *7,* was shelled and sunk. Cameron with his crew of three and Place with only one other survivor were taken prisoner on the ship they had crippled; they were treated in a way that did credit to their heroism. *X-10* was scuttled on its return journey as it was found to have the same defects as its companion submarines. It had missed *Scharnhorst,* its intended victim, because the battle-cruiser was engaged in target practice off the Altenfjord, but it lost nothing by waiting.

On December 22 a Luftwaffe reconnaissance plane spotted an enemy convoy 465 miles west of Tromsö; in fact this was J.W. 55B, which consisted of 19 merchant ships and ten destroyers; it was due to pass R.A. 55A, bringing back 21 empty ships from Murmansk, in the neighbourhood of Bear Island. Vice-Admiral Burnett was responsible for protecting this two-way passage with the heavy cruiser *Norfolk* and the light cruisers *Sheffield* and *Belfast*. In order to provide greater cover, Sir Bruce Fraser, flying his flag on the battleship *Duke of York,* with the light cruiser *Jamaica* and four destroyers, sailed from the Akureyri, the Allied base on the north coast of Iceland, on December 23.

When it received the first signal of an enemy convoy, the German naval group at Kåfjord, as whose commander Rear-Admiral E. Bey had just succeeded Vice-Admiral O. Kummetz, had been put at the alert; on the evening of December 25 it

△ △ *Captain F. J. Walker, commander of the 2nd Escort Group, comes ashore from his sloop* Starling.
△ *Lieutenant-Commander P. W. Gretton, who led the B7 Escort Group with Convoy S.C. 130. On the Atlantic crossing from St. Johns to Londonderry between May 14 and 20, five U-boats were sunk.*

British submarines. Although they had little or no German commerce on which to prey, the Mediterranean offered the possibilities of the Italian merchant marine, and the Pacific such Japanese shipping that the U.S. submarine arm had left. Operations against Germany consisted mostly of patrols to detect and intercept major warships as they left harbour.

△ Alongside a depôt ship. On the right is the "S"-class Stygian, *with another "S" beside her and the "T"-class* Tudor *on the left.*

◁ *Part of another British flotilla. On the left is a "T"-class boat, with inside her the "S"-class* Subtle, *a "V"-class, and another "S".*

▷ △ *A 21-inch torpedo is lowered from a depôt ship to one of her flotilla.*

▷ ▷ *The submarine depôt ship* Forth, *with a torpedo being hoisted from one of her store rooms for a submarine of the 3rd Flotilla.*

▷ *A submarine of the "T"-class.*

was ordered to attack the convoy. A few hours later, a message from Dönitz arrived to confirm its mission:

"1. By sending the Russians a large consignment of food supplies and *matériel,* the enemy is trying to make our army's heroic struggles on the Eastern Front even more difficult. We must go to the help of our soldiers.

2. Attack the convoy with *Scharnhorst* and destroyers."

Though the mission was clear, the Grand-Admiral followed it with contradictory instructions. Bey should not be satisfied with a "half-success", but should seize the opportunity of "attacking in force". Nevertheless he was allowed the option of breaking off the engagement, and he was reminded that the "essential thing" was always to avoid any "engagement against superior forces".

While he was pursuing the enemy, Bey was foolhardy enough to break radio silence; and so the Admiralty was able to signal Fraser that *Scharnhorst* was probably at sea. At approximately 0400 on December 26 the Home Fleet commander ordered convoy J.W. 55B to withdraw to the north, with Vice-Admiral Burnett covering its withdrawal. Fraser himself increased to 24 knots to close *Scharnhorst,* which he placed about 250 to 275 miles from *Duke of York.*

At 0840 *Belfast's* radar identified a large enemy warship about 20 miles to the north-west and at 0924, at a distance of eight miles, *Belfast* fired her first star-shell, illuminating *Scharnhorst.* During a brief engagement, *Norfolk,* without being hit, obtained two direct hits with 8-inch shells and destroyed the radar rangefinder in *Scharnhorst's* bows. Bey withdrew, doubtless hoping to circle round the British detachment and attack the convoy which, it will be recalled, was his chief target. This manoeuvre was frustrated by Burnett, who in the meantime had requested the convoy to lend him four destroyers. These moves led to a second engagement at approximately 1230, and this time the light favoured the battle-cruiser; one of her 11-inch shells put *Norfolk's* aft gun-turret out of action, whilst *Sheffield* was covered with shell splinters.

In spite of this success, the German admiral retreated for the second time at a speed of 28 knots. In his memoirs, Dönitz shows moderation in his comments on the movements of his unfortunate sub-

ordinate, but clearly they do not meet with his approval. However, it is only fair to point out that Bey kept strictly to Dönitz's instruction not to endanger his ship; he would have disobeyed this order had he ventured further with his radar not functioning in the half-light of the Arctic day. On the other hand a message from a plane was signalled to him at 1100: "Five ships north-west of North Cape". As none of Scharnhorst's 36 survivors had a hand in the decision which was to lead to its destruction, one must be careful in one's comments.

When he headed for his base at about 1430, the German admiral, who was pursued by Burnett at the limit of radar range, had no idea that he was about to meet the Home Fleet; moreover he did not know that the plane message received at 1100 had an important passage missing: "Including probably one heavy ship". In fact, at 1617 Scharnhorst appeared on Duke of York's radar screen 25½ miles to the north-north-east, approaching rapidly. At 1650 the English warship, at a range of less than 6½ miles, opened fire on her adversary, who was lit up by Belfast's star-shells. Total surprise was achieved. The German battle-cruiser tur-

ned north again, and then meeting Burnett, tried to escape in an easterly direction. During this engagement she had been hit by three 14-inch shells; one of them exploded in a boiler room, and another put the forward 11-inch turret out of action. Although disabled, Scharnhorst managed to break contact at 1820; Duke of York had ceased fire when Sir Bruce Fraser's four destroyers attacked Scharnhorst on both sides. Although she managed to avoid Scorpion's and Stord's torpedoes, she laid herself open to the wave of 12 torpedoes launched at her by Savage and Saumarez at point-blank range. Three hit their mark a little before 1850, and half an hour later Bey signalled: "We shall fight to the last shell."

Crushed by Duke of York's shells and all the light ships' torpedoes, Scharnhorst sank at 1945 on December 26. The victors picked up only 36 out of a crew of just under 1,900 men; both Rear-Admiral Bey and his flag captain, Captain Hintze, were lost. According to Roskill, thirteen 14-inch shells and 11 torpedoes were necessary to sink this heroic ship. "Once again the ability of the Germans to build tremendously stout ships had been demonstrated."

◁△ *The* King George V-*class battleship* Duke of York. *Opening fire at long range by radar, she soon slowed* Scharnhorst *with a hit in a boiler room. This long range fire proved to be the decisive factor in the battle–Duke of York's 14-inch shells, plunging steeply down from the top of their high trajectory, were too much for* Scharnhorst's *deck armour.*

◁◁ *The British light cruiser* Sheffield.

◁▽ Scharnhorst *at sea. Visible here is part of the turreted secondary armament of 5.9-inch guns, with four of the 4.1-inch A.A. guns above them and a pair of 3.7-cm A.A. guns in the foreground.*

△ *"The Sinking of the* Scharnhorst" *by C. E. Turner.*

1942

February

15. Singapore surrenders, Allied losses in campaign 9,000 killed, 130,000 captured.
19. Japanese invade Bali, bomb Darwin.
20. U.S. grants billion dollar loan to U.S.S.R.
21. Rommel launches offensive against 8th Army.
22. MacArthur ordered to leave Philippines, appointed C.-in-C. Allied Forces in Australia.
25. Dissolution of A.B.D.A. Command.
27. Battle of the Java Sea; Allied force destroyed by Japanese.
28. Japanese invade Java.
28-29. Action off Bantem Bay, with loss of *Exeter*.

March

5. Alexander becomes G.O.C. Burma.
9. Yamashita appointed C.-in-C. Philippines. Dutch East Indies government capitulates.
10. Stilwell appointed Chief-of-Staff in China.
11. MacArthur leaves Corregidor.
18. Mountbatten appointed Chief of Combined Operations.

28-29. Raid on St. Nazaire: *Campbeltown* rams and demolishes lock gate.
29. India offered full Dominion status after war in proposed Constitutional changes.

April

1. Japanese begin landings in Dutch New Guinea.
3. Massive assault by Japanese on last line defences in Bataan.
4. Submarine *Upholder* lost in Mediterranean.
5. Congress of Slavic peoples in Moscow. Cruisers *Dorsetshire* and *Cornwall* sunk by Japanese.
9. Gandhi arrested. King surrenders on Bataan. *Hermes* sunk in Indian Ocean.
16. George Cross awarded to Malta. Indian Congress party refuses terms offered by Cripps Mission.
18. Doolittle raid on Tokyo.
27. Roosevelt outlines war economy measures.
29. Hitler and Mussolini meet at Salzburg.
30. Japanese complete conquest of central Burma.

May

1. British evacuate Mandalay.
5. British land on Madagascar. Japanese land on Corregidor.
6. 11,500 men of the Corregidor garrison surrender.
7. Battle of the Coral Sea. Japanese lose the carrier *Shoho*.
8. U.S.N. loses the *Lexington* in the main action of Coral Sea battle. Manstein begins offensive in the Crimea: 150,000 Russian casualties.
11. Zionist congress in Washington discusses foundation of Jewish state in Palestine.
12. R.A.F. shoots down 13 German troop transports off N. African coast.
13. Russians launch strong attack in Khar'kov area, and retreat in Kerch' peninsula.
15. Russo-Japanese agreement on Manchuria and Mongolia. British forces cross Burma-India frontier.
20. Germans recapture the Kerch' peninsula. Japanese take up defensive positions in Burma.
28. Germans destroy large Russian forces near Khar'kov. Tank battle

at Bir Hakeim. Mexico declares war on the Axis.
29. Bomb attack on Heydrich in Prague.
30. First 1,000-bomber raid, target Cologne.
31. Fierce fighting in the "Cauldron" at Gazala.

June

4. Heydrich dies of wounds.
4-5. Japan loses *Soryu, Akagi, Kaga,* and *Hiryu* in Battle of Midway. U.S.N. loses *Yorktown*.
5. Germans begin the siege of Sevastopol'.
7. Germans attack Bir Hakeim. Assault on Sevastopol'. Japanese invade Aleutians.
10. Lidice destroyed in German

retaliation after Heydrich's death. Free French withdraw from Bir Hakeim.

13. Ritchie orders withdrawal of 8th Army.

14-30. Retreat into Egypt.

16. One of two convoys reaches Malta after heavy air attacks.

19. Churchill, Roosevelt confer on the second front and the atomic bomb.

21. Tobruk falls. Germans drive wedge into Sevastopol' defences.

26. Rommel promoted to Field-Marshal.

28. British withdraw to El Alamein area. Germans launch offensive in Kursk area.

30. Rommel reaches El Alamein.

July

3. The Axis declares it will respect Egypt's independence after her liberation. Sevastopol' falls after heroic defence.

4. Convoy P.Q.-17 attacked by German aircraft. Convoy scatters. 23 ships lost in subsequent attacks by U-boats and aircraft.

12. Australians reach Kokoda.

21. Leahy appointed Chief-of-Staff to Roosevelt.

28. Germans capture Rostov.

31. Germans cross Don on 150-mile front.

August

4-9. Paulus begins his drive on Stalingrad.

7. U.S. Marines land on Guadal-

canal and Tulagi.

9. Battle of Savo Island. Germans capture Krasnodar and Maykop.

11. Fierce attacks on "Pedestal" convoy to Malta.

12. First Moscow Conference. Churchill and Stalin discuss the Second Front. Cruiser *Cairo* lost in Mediterranean.

13. Montgomery takes command of the 8th Army. Cruiser *Manchester* lost.

17. Germans establish bridgeheads in the Kuban' peninsula.

18-19. British and Canadians raid Dieppe with very heavy losses.

20. The Germans reach the Volga. *Gebirgsjägers* scale Mount El'brus. U.S. aircraft arrive at Henderson Field on Guadalcanal.

28. Fierce fighting around Stalingrad. Japanese troops halted at Milne Bay.

31. The Battle of Alam el Halfa begins.

September

3. New Zealanders attack at Alam el Halfa.

7. Japanese forces withdrawn from Milne Bay. Line stabilised at Alam el Halfa.

9. Germans order conscription in Alsace-Lorraine.

17. Japanese halted at Ioribawa on the Owen Stanley Ridge in New Guinea.

25. R.A.F. makes low level attack in daylight on Gestapo H.Q. at Oslo.

26. Australians counter-attack on Imita Ridge in New Guinea.

October

11-12. Battle of Cape Esperance off Guadalcanal.

14. Australians meet stubborn resistance on the Kokoda Trail. Loss of cruiser *Coventry* in Mediterranean.

23-25. Land battle of Guadalcanal.

23. Battle of El Alamein begins.

25-26. Battle of Santa Cruz. U.S.N. loses the *Hornet*.

25. Alamein offensive grows more intense.

26. Heavy fighting in Stalingrad.

27. The 8th Army regroups for the final breakthrough at Alamein.

30. Australians renew their attacks at Alamein.

November

1. Heavy fighting on Guadalcanal.
2. Operation "Supercharge" opens at Alamein. Japanese land men and supplies at Tetere.
4. Start of Axis retreat from Alamein.
8. Operation "Torch": Allied forces land in Algeria and Morocco. Roosevelt broadcasts to the French.
8-9. French resistance to landings at Casablanca and Oran.
11. Axis troops invade unoccupied France. The Darlan Incident – Admiral Darlan agrees to co-operate with the Allies.
19. Red Army opens winter offensive. Pincer attacks on Stalingrad.
23. 6th Army surrounded at Stalingrad.
27. German troops enter Toulon. French scuttle fleet according to plan.
28. Soviet offensive liberates huge areas of Russia.

December

2. Professor Fermi sets up atomic reactor in Chicago. Beveridge Report on Social Security issued in U.K.
9. Relief of 1st Marine Division at Guadalcanal.
12. Germans launch counter-attack to relieve Stalingrad.
13. Rommel retreats from El Agheila.
18. Australian and U.S. troops in fierce fighting on Papua. Manstein's counter-attack is halted.
24. Darlan assassinated.
28. Hitler agrees to withdraw Army Group "A" from Caucasus.

January

3. Germans start withdrawal from Caucasus.
5. Mark Clark appointed U.S. 5th Army Commander.
8. Rokossovsky sends surrender demand to 6th Army at Stalingrad.
10. Meeting between Hitler and Antonescu.
14-23. Casablanca Conference.
18. Russian attack at Leningrad.
27. First U.S.A.A.F. attack on Germany.
31. Paulus capitulates at Stalingrad.

February

1-8. Japanese evacuation of Guadalcanal.
2. Remaining German forces at Stalingrad surrender.
2-20. Russians drive across the Donets.
5. Mussolini dismisses Ciano and Grandi.
14-22. Battle of Kasserine.
17. Guderian appointed Inspector of Panzers.
18. 77th Brigade (the Chindits) cross the Chindwin. Manstein begins counter-offensive.
28. Norwegian commandos destroy heavy water installations.

March

2-4. Battle of the Bismarck Sea.
7. Rommel leaves Africa.
14. Khark'kov recaptured by the Germans.
18. The Chindits cross the Irrawaddy.
20-26. The Battle of Mareth.
26. Battle of Komandorski Islands.
31. Russians advance in the Kuban'.

April

1-22. Axis withdrawal in North Africa.
6. 8th Army attacks at Wadi Akarit.
7. Patton links up with Montgomery.
18. Death of Yamamoto, shot down by U.S. fighters.
19. Rising in Warsaw Ghetto as Germans move to clear remaining Jews.

21. Washington discloses that Japanese have beheaded U.S. airmen captured in Tokyo raid.
23. Hitler orders "utmost severity" in Warsaw operations.

May

1. Germans driven from Jefna.
3. Mateur captured by U.S. II Corps. Germans counter-attack in Kuban'.
3-13. The Battle of Tunisia.
7. U.S. 34th Div. enters Bizerta. British 7th Armoured Div. enters Tunis.
11. Axis forces start to surrender on Cape Bon. Final count 275,000 prisoners.
11-29. U.S. forces recapture Attu in the Aleutians. 29 of the 2,500 garrison are captured.
12. Arnim surrenders; the end of the *Afrika Korps*.
15-25. Trident Conferences in Washington.